New Happy

Getting Happiness Right in a World That's Got It Wrong

STEPHANIE HARRISON

W0008587

First published in the United States in 2024 by TarcherPerigee, an imprint of
Penguin Random House LLC
First published in Great Britain in 2024 by Orion Spring,
an imprint of The Orion Publishing Group Ltd
Carmelite House, 50 Victoria Embankment
London EC4Y 0DZ
An Hachette UK Company

10 9 8 7 6 5 4 3

A CIP catalogue record for this book is available from the British Library.

ISBN (Hardback) 978 1 3987 2208 8
ISBN (Export Trade Paperback) 978 1 3987 2212 5
ISBN (eBook) 978 1 3987 2209 5
ISBN (Audio) 978 1 3987 2210 1

Printed and bound in Italy by L.E.G.O. S.p.A.

MIX
Paper | Supporting
responsible forestry
FSC
www.fsc.org   FSC® C104740

www.orionbooks.co.uk

While the author has made every effort to provide accurate
telephone numbers, internet addresses, and other contact information
at the time of publication, neither the publisher nor the author assume
any responsibility for errors or for changes that occur after publication.
Further, the publisher does not have any control over and does not
assume any responsibility for author or third-party websites or their content.

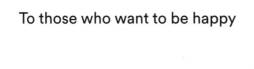

To those who want to be happy

Contents

PART FOUR
Uncover Your Gifts

PART FIVE
Serve the World

Introduction:
My Story

I don't know how long I lay there, curled up in a ball on my bedroom floor, crying. It was 2013, and I could see a sliver of the sun setting as darkness softly spread across New York City. It felt like the darkness was spreading within me, too.

And then, out of nowhere, I felt a new and very different emotion. I felt curious.

It was very *curious* that I was so deeply, desperately unhappy. Because everyone had told me that I was doing all of the right things, all of the things that would make me happy.

But in reality, I was unbearably lonely. I had daily panic attacks, developed a stress-induced autoimmune disease, and felt an overwhelming sense of hopelessness almost every day.

"I wonder why that is," I thought. Then I went back to crying.

I did not know that this moment of curiosity would end up changing my life forever.

Since I was little, I have wanted to be happy. Yet no matter how hard I tried, happiness always eluded me. It felt like I was always chasing something that was just around the corner, contingent upon the next achievement:

"If you can be better looking . . .

"If you can be thinner . . .

"If you can get good grades . . .

"If you can make lots of friends . . .

"If you can get people to like you . . .

"If you can please everyone . . .

"If you can get into the right school . . .

"If you can get the best job . . .

"If you can be the best at that job . . .

"If you can do more, more, more . . .

. . . then you will be happy."

Did I listen to the whispers? You bet I did. Did I strive for more, more, more? I did, and then some. It seemed like an irrevocable law: achieve these things and then you will be happy. I could see that the law was working for everyone else, with their jobs and partners and parties and smiles. Obviously, they had figured out something that I hadn't. There had to be something wrong with *me*.

I doubled down on my beliefs, trying even harder to become the perfect person who achieved all of the approved goals in a flawless manner at exactly the right time. Any day now, I was sure of it, things would change. And while my life—getting into a great university, excelling in my classes, landing a prestigious job, living in a nice apartment—became something that other people applauded and celebrated, it never made me happy.

I kept looking around the corner. Surely my happiness was waiting for me after the *next* achievement. My problem was that I was in the wrong job, or I wasn't getting promoted fast enough, or I lived in the wrong place. If I kept working hard enough and achieved this perfect existence, I would be able to stop running and finally be happy.

That spark of curiosity during my weepy eureka moment on my bedroom floor was the first time I ever questioned my deepest belief about what happiness was and how to pursue it. It was time to throw out my old playbook and try something new.

Slowly, I started making changes in my life: moving from New York to San Francisco, finding a more meaningful job, and cultivating healthier relationships. And I started studying happiness, reading everything I could to understand where I had gone wrong. I kept wondering: Was I alone in chasing after a completely misguided definition of happiness, or was this something that other people had experienced, too?

As it happened, my existential crisis coincided with the rise of a new academic discipline, positive psychology, which studied human happiness. In 2015, I enrolled in a master's program at the University of Pennsylvania (apparently still intent on getting into the right school), where I wrote a thesis arguing that we had gotten our definition of happiness all wrong. I proposed a new definition, one that was grounded in the pursuit of love, service, and our common humanity. It was the beginning of the book that you hold in your hands now.

After completing my degree, I planned to continue my research by pursuing a PhD in psychology. But life had other plans for me.

In the winter of 2017, I met and fell madly, head over heels in love with a man named Alex. He was an artist, a designer, an athlete, a visionary; passionate, kind, and brilliant. I had never met anyone before who was so *alive*. Alex crackled with energy, possessed by an overwhelming desire to use every minute well. Just before we met, he had rekindled his childhood passion for skateboarding. He'd sneak out of bed at 5 a.m. to go practice, climbing the wire fence to get into the still-closed skatepark as the sun was coming up. Three hours later,

I'd wake up and find him bounding back into the apartment, drenched in sweat and full of joy. Like me, he dreamed of a better world. We would spend our weekends walking around San Francisco, drinking too many cups of coffee, and planning how we would make our world a more beautiful place.

And then, less than a year after we met, Alex got sick. I don't mean sick with the flu. He was sick with something mysterious and undiagnosable, something no doctor could figure out.

Alex went from being a healthy, independent man to someone who couldn't care for himself in any way. During the next four years, we experienced a series of escalating heartbreaks. He went from exercising and skateboarding seven days a week to being unable to walk around the block, to being unable to leave the apartment, to being unable to get out of bed. I have never seen someone fight harder to get well, to keep his job, and to merely persevere through each day. Eventually, he was left spending his days lying alone in the dark, unable to bear another human being's presence, subjected to never-ending physical pain and a fatigue that was so crushing, all he could do was try to keep existing. His body was present, but the Alex I knew and loved had disappeared.

I was so naive. I thought that if you went to the doctor with an illness, they would find a way to fix you. It turns out it doesn't work that way if you have a chronic, mysterious illness here in the United States.

My plan to pursue a PhD faded away as I became Alex's full-time caregiver, medical detective, and advocate. Instead of pursuing my own studies, I spent my nights researching rare diseases. On lunch breaks I pored through online medical forums, managed Alex's dizzying array of medications, and cold-emailed strangers who were equally lost in the wilderness of their own medical mysteries. On my vacation days I took Alex to doctors with eight-month waiting lists and begged them for their help, only to be met with confusion or outright disbelief that a healthy young man could find himself declining in this way. Alex was told that it was all in his head, that if he became more positive and forced himself to exercise, he'd eventually "get back to normal." I was laughed at by doctors who rolled their eyes at my binder of test results, requests for specific exams, and chronology of his symptoms.

Each month brought new drugs and experimental treatments but no answers. And each day I watched helplessly as the man I loved wasted away.

THE NEW HAPPY

I was engaged in an uphill struggle to save Alex's life. The reality of this made my previous challenges back in New York seem like child's play.

But now, five years later, something was different: I had my new set of beliefs and tools, and I realized they were good for life's ups *and* downs. I had learned a new definition of happiness academically; now life was giving me a chance to put that knowledge to the test. It turned out that it worked not only in scientific studies, but in the real world, too. In the midst of suffering, at what, by any external measure, was a low point of my life, I was able to find happiness—albeit a fundamentally different kind of happiness from the version my younger self had sought.

It was shocking to compare my 2013 self, who had everything going "right" and yet felt lost, miserable, and isolated, to my 2018 self, who had everything going "wrong" and yet felt far more peace, joy, and purpose.

I felt like I was onto something. My next, and most important, question was: Would this philosophy work for others?

In 2018, I took my graduate thesis and started The New Happy as a free weekly newsletter, sharing insights, tips, and stories. The first email went to about seventeen people.

Slowly, I kept writing, and slowly, people kept subscribing. As I sent The New Happy out into the world, I got the answer to my question. I was *not* alone—not at all. People everywhere were tired of chasing an empty definition of happiness that left them even less fulfilled. Like me, they were hungry for something different. The incredible response gave me a purpose.

By 2020, Alex had become so ill that caring for him had become a full-time job. I decided to leave my role as director of learning at Thrive Global, where I was leading the development of programs that helped employees at the world's biggest companies be healthy and happy.

I tried my best to see it as an opportunity: in the space around my caregiving role, I could spend more time helping people through The New Happy. It was three months into the pandemic, and people were struggling. I decided to take all I had discovered and share it, in every medium I could—writing articles, making art, starting a podcast, delivering training programs—all delivered for free to anyone who needed it.

In truth, I needed it for myself, too. Everything I created was helping me as much as it was helping others. I wrote and sketched in doctor's offices and hospitals and before and after injecting Alex with drugs and tracking his symptoms. I jotted down ideas on my phone with one hand, while I used the other to hold his hand at his bedside. I came up with tools to use for my darkest days and passed them on in hopes that others would find them useful. Alex helped me along the way, too, in the few moments of health he had, fighting to contribute even as he struggled to get through each day. Whenever I wanted to give up, I thought about how, in the depths of such suffering, he still tried to help make the world better in some way.

The New Happy grew beyond my wildest dreams. It became a thriving community of nearly a million people (many of whose stories are shared in these pages) but also a bigger movement striving to create collective happiness in the world around us. Our work has been used in elementary and high schools, universities, homes, prisons, governments, companies, hospitals, treatment centers, and therapy offices all over the world.

Here's what I now know for sure: you have the power to change your life and find lasting happiness.

WHAT YOU WILL LEARN

In this book, you'll find a step-by-step guide to the New Happy philosophy of happiness.

Philosophy is a big word. It might conjure up images of someone sitting alone in a library pondering deep thoughts or a high-minded ideal that's impossible for the average person to embody. That is not what you'll find in this book. The New Happy philosophy is *a way of living*. It's something you do, and it's accessible for each and every one of us. You might be surprised to discover that New Happy is so easy to live and yet can have a disproportionately powerful impact on your happiness.

A quick word about my approach. It's based in interdisciplinary scholarship, a method I was trained in as an undergraduate student at New York University. You define a core topic or key question—in this case, it is "How can we find lasting happiness?"—and then explore it from different perspectives.

This approach can lead to fascinating new insights because it breaks the traditional academic norm. Usually, we look at topics through narrow lenses: when a psychologist looks at happiness, they primarily focus on the individual; when a sociologist looks at happiness, they focus on the environment; when an economist looks at happiness, they focus on work and income; and so on. This is an excellent way to delve deeply into specific topics.

But for a subject like happiness, I think we need to take a step back and look at the bigger picture. I believe one of the reasons we're struggling so much with happiness is because we have been neglecting this complexity. To get a fuller picture, I've studied and incorporated the findings of experts in sociology, philosophy, psychology, economics, history, anthropology, religion, education, biology, social work, art, literature, business, design, and politics. In fact, this book has so many hundreds of references that we couldn't print them at the end—they would have made the book far too long! Please visit thenewhappy .com/bookreferences, where you can review the references, read detailed notes, and find additional reading recommendations.

The philosophy I'll be describing in this book might feel both bold and familiar at the same time. It's bold because it's very different from what we have been told. It's familiar because it is aligned with our deepest nature.

HOW TO USE THIS BOOK

I have one request for you as you read. And one wish.

First, my request: You probably found this book in your bookstore or library's self-help section (which, as you'll discover later, is ironic). This tells me that you're a person who wants to be happy. It also tells me that you're someone with an open mind, a person who wants to grow and transform. Some of the ideas in this book don't merely run counter to what we've been taught; they're ones that the powers of our society don't want us to even think about. Please explore these ideas and test them out for yourself. You know what is best for you. I hope you'll take this philosophy and make it your own.

And my wish: My greatest, most wildly ambitious wish is that this book rings a bell inside you. I hope that bell peals so loudly that it shakes all of the false messages from where they have settled in the rafters of your heart and they come crashing down once and for all. I hope there, in the open space that remains, you discover what happiness truly means to you.

PART ONE

The Happiness Myth

1

How We Got It All So Wrong

There was once a man who wanted to be happy.

His childhood had been difficult. His parents didn't seem to love him. His father, especially, was cruel to him, constantly pointing out all of the ways in which he was not good enough. At school, he was left out and teased. He escaped into his favorite books, looking for comfort in their heroic tales and fantastic realms. He was determined that one day, when he was grown up, he'd leave behind all this pain and be happy.

First, he had to figure out how to do that. He looked at the world around him to learn what he needed to do to be happy, and the answer was clear: become successful, powerful, and wealthy.

He began working very hard, quickly becoming a leader in his business. His choices had a cost, though. His mind would spin, day and night, tossing his worries around and around: Was he doing enough? How could he get more? His fiancée eventually broke up with him, tiring of his growing obsession. He justified his choices to himself: "Soon, I will get there, and then I will be happy, and then I can make it up to everyone."

He miserably pursued happiness.

Yet no matter how hard he worked and how much he gained, happiness eluded him. His pain made him angry, mean, and cynical, and as time passed, he grew more and more isolated.

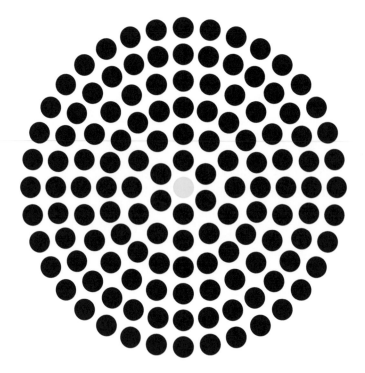

Every single one of us wants to find happiness.
It is at the center of everything we do.

But then, one day many years later, a miracle happened. He woke up, and *he was happy*!

What happened? Did he finally "get there," achieving the specific, elusive level of success that would guarantee happiness?

Or was it something else? If so, what could possibly change this man's life, after so many years of misery, in such a powerful way?

HAPPINESS DRIVES EVERYTHING WE DO

We all want to be happy: this man, you, me, and everyone we know.

Happiness is the single most important goal in a human being's life. It drives everything you do. Every goal you set. Every decision you make. Every action you take. They all ladder up to it, seeking a way to make you happier, whether it's in the short term or the long term:

- The breakfast you picked up this morning
- The job you're interviewing for
- The exercise program you're starting
- The person you're dating
- Your weekend plans
- Your career aspirations
- Your big life goals

They all promise happiness in some form or another. It's like we're being guided by a compass inside us, one that is always pointed toward our version of true north—happiness.

In one study across forty-seven nations, students ranked happiness as "extraordinarily important," the single most important goal in their life.

In our brains, circuits help us pursue what we think will make us happy. When we want something, our brain kicks off a motivational process that compels us to set out and pursue it. When we get that thing, we experience a surge of positive, pleasurable feelings. Over time, this process teaches us that certain things reliably will make us feel good, thus inspiring us to want to pursue them again.

People show up in therapy and say, "I just want to be happy." Parents describe their dearest hope for their children as, "I want them to be happy." We say it to ourselves when we're trying to make a decision: "What choice will make me happy?"

This validates what William James, the father of American psychology, wrote back in 1902: "How to gain, how to keep, how to recover happiness is in fact for most men at all times the secret motive for all they do."

Up until now, your happiness compass has probably been invisible to you. If you take a step back from your daily behaviors and choices, though, you can start to notice it. The best way to do it is to get in touch with your inner toddler and ask yourself, "*Why* did I make that decision?"

Say you're frustrated at work and thinking about leaving your job.

- Why are you considering that? Because it is creating a lot of stress in your life.
- Why is it creating stress for you? Because the job is not a good fit for you.
- Why isn't it a good fit for you? Because you're not getting to do what you're best at.
- Why do you want to do what you're best at? Because you think it will make you happy.

Or imagine that you're trying to choose what to do after high school.

- Why do you want to go to college? Because it will help you learn a valuable skill.
- Why do you want to learn a valuable skill? Because it will help you get a good job after graduating.
- Why do you want to get a good job after graduating? Because it will help you earn lots of money.
- Why do you want to earn lots of money? Because you will be able to buy all of the things that you want.

- Why do you want to buy all of the things that you want?
  Because it will make you happy.

Eventually, if you ask "Why?" enough times, you will hit the deepest, driving desire: happiness. As the French philosopher and mathematician Blaise Pascal said, "All men seek happiness. This is without exception. Whatever different means they employ, they all tend to this end. The cause of some going to war and of others avoiding it, is the same desire in both, attended with different views."

Yet despite happiness being our most important goal, so many of us are unhappy. Studies find that Americans are the unhappiest they've been in fifty years. One in three Americans are lonely. Twenty percent of Americans are dealing with a mental illness, and in one recent survey, 76 percent of working Americans reported at least one symptom of a mental health condition. Between 2000 and 2018, suicide rates grew by 35 percent.

If the pursuit of happiness drives every single thing that we do, why are we *so miserable*?

YOUR DEFINITION OF HAPPINESS

To answer this question, let's return to the man from the beginning of this chapter. You have met him before and heard his story many times, only told in a different way.

This man's name is Ebenezer Scrooge. He's the famously miserable man who spreads gloom all around him but who is, deep down, someone who just wants to be happy, like you and me.

Scrooge's only problem was that he had a bad definition of happiness. It led him to make choices that made himself and others miserable.

You might be wondering what a definition of happiness is and how changing it could possibly have such a huge impact. You'd be right to do so, given it's something we rarely discuss. Before that day crying on my bedroom floor, I wouldn't have known how I defined happiness either. My definition was so embedded that I took it for granted as the truth. It never once occurred to me that it was an idea, something that could be changed.

Our definition is so important because happiness is a fuzzy, vague concept. We all know what it feels like, but it's not something we can point to, like a chair or a flower or a snail. Philosophers and scientists have been squabbling over what happiness is for thousands of years, proposing hundreds of different definitions.

When you look up happiness in the dictionary, the word is defined as "a state of well-being and contentment." Not helpful. If happiness drives everything we do, we need to have an idea of what will lead to this state.

In the absence of a clear definition, we look to the world to tell us what happiness is. This definition gets documented in our own personal dictionary of beliefs:

This will make me happy.

From there, this definition guides all of the decisions that you make and the actions that you take in your lifelong pursuit of happiness.

When Scrooge's dead business partner, Jacob Marley, and the three ghosts visited him on Christmas, he was shocked into realizing how wrong his definition of happiness was.

He suddenly could see it all so clearly. The path of money and success—pursuits stemming from a deep place of not feeling good enough, which lead to isolation—would never make him happy. If he continued living in this way, he would die alone and unloved, a loss only remarked upon with exclamations of relief.

Desperately, Scrooge pleaded with the Ghost of Christmas Yet to Come, "Assure me that I yet may change these shadows you have shown me, by an altered life!"

Scrooge was given a second chance. He took it. He woke up and began living in a brand-new way. His neighbors didn't recognize him because no one had ever seen him smiling. With one choice, he changed his whole life, and he went from being the most miserable

Society has distorted our understanding of happiness,
convincing us to pursue all of the wrong things.

man around to becoming "as good a friend, as good a master, and as good a man, as the good old city knew, or any other good old city, town, or borough, in the good old world."

We know this story as a fable, but I think we should look at it in another light: a cautionary tale. When I ask people about how they were taught to define happiness, I get remarkably similar answers. Scrooge just took them to the extreme.

The world has told us that happiness comes from:

- Being perfect, or as close to it as possible
- Making more and more money
- Acquiring more and more stuff
- Conforming to the prescribed path
- Working harder and harder (and never resting or slowing down)
- Gaining fame, popularity, and acclaim
- Competing against other people (and winning)

This is Old Happy—our society's broken definition of happiness that is, in fact, the very source of our deep unhappiness.

As it turns out, none of these things make us happy. Studies show that perfectionism is a leading cause of depression and anxiety. The more you value getting lots of stuff, the more your well-being decreases. Overworking significantly harms your physical and mental health. Denying who you really are and what matters to you leads to ill-being. The pursuit of goals like fame and fortune often prevents you from fulfilling your true psychological needs of authenticity and connection. Viewing life as a competition increases stress and loneliness.

In a recent podcast interview, Shaquille O'Neal—one of the most recognizable figures in sports and culture, whose long list of accomplishments includes multiple National Basketball Association (NBA) most valuable player (MVP) honors and four NBA championships—described an extreme manifestation of Old Happy: "I live in a thirty-thousand-square-foot house by myself. You don't think I know I messed up?"

If you're wondering whether Old Happy has infiltrated your life, see if any of these statements from our community members resonate with you:

"I never feel like I'm good enough."

"I got what I thought I wanted. I still feel miserable."

"I never let myself take breaks or rest."

"It feels like I'm pretending to be someone I'm not."

"I feel so lonely all of the time."

"Am I the only one who is secretly miserable but pretending not to be?"

"I'm doing what I'm 'supposed' to do. Why isn't it working?"

We build our lives around the pursuit of Old Happy. We push ourselves harder and harder to achieve it. We craft a culture that encourages, incentivizes, and forces it. And, tragically, many of us die having never really been happy, sold a false bill of goods but holding out hope until the end that somehow, we'll "get there."

However, like Scrooge, we can change our definition before it's too late. I'm here to be the Ghost of Happiness Yet to Come, to show you how your definition of happiness might be leading you astray and to give you the tools, science, and support to redefine happiness and live the life you deserve.

LASTING HAPPINESS IS POSSIBLE

For the last ten years, one question has consumed me: What is a better definition of happiness? As I read thousands of academic studies and hundreds of books by philosophers and theologians and artists and leaders, I traced two threads that appeared again and again: you need to be yourself, and you need to give of yourself.

I discovered that same message, written in different words by different people. For example, Mary Shelley, the author of *Frankenstein*, wrote, "There is but one solution to the intricate riddle of life, to improve ourselves and contribute to the happiness of others."

In every tradition and discipline, people were describing it. Marie Curie, winner of two Nobel Prizes, wrote, "Each of us must work for his own improvement, and at the same time share a general responsibility for all humanity, our particular duty being to aid those to whom we think we can be most useful."

Our most beloved leaders and cherished icons championed it, as when Martin Luther King Jr. said, "Those who are not looking for happiness are the most likely to find it, because those who are searching forget that the surest way to be happy is to seek happiness for others."

I traced these threads through the science, too. Studies show that using your unique strengths makes you feel happier, helps you grow, and offers a venue for self-expression. People who are connected to others live longer, happier lives. Integrating the two leads to a sense of meaning and purpose, makes an impact on the world, and provides you with the feeling that your life matters.

Here was the answer to my question: to be happy, discover who you are and share yourself in ways that help other people. *This* is the path to happiness, and I call it New Happy.

In some ways, it's not really new. Many years ago, people like Aristotle and the Buddha were advocating for something similar. However, not only were their ideas hard enough to apply at the time, but our world has changed dramatically since then. They also didn't have access to what we have: the wonders of modern science, which have helped us confirm many of their insights but also take them much, much further. The New Happy philosophy has been shaped by their wisdom but is grounded in modern research and expanded to address our real-life needs.

Contrary to what we've been taught, happiness isn't something that you have to acquire, or wait for, or please someone else to receive.

Happiness isn't found in any of Old Happy's haunts, and you don't need a haunting to find it for yourself.

The transformation that Scrooge undergoes is not merely a children's story. It's something that's possible for you, too. You can have moments of joy, that build to days of fulfillment, that make a life that leaves people better off because you existed. When you change your definition of happiness, everything else changes, too.

WE CAN FIX THIS

If you have been living by Old Happy, I need you to know something: *it's not your fault.* As you'll learn in the next chapter, your definition of happiness has been handed to you by society. You never even had a chance to choose.

We believe what we have been taught: we trust our teachers and preachers and caregivers and what they tell us to be and do. Then, unless we learn differently, we pass it on. We teach those beliefs to our own kids, friends, and community. That's how these ideas end up sticking around, enshrined as truth, even without evidence.

Old Happy is only one of many things we've believed through the years that turned out to be wrong.

We believed that our planet was the center of the universe. Then we learned that the earth revolves around the sun.

We believed that kings and queens were chosen by the gods and had the power to rule over all other humans. Then we created democracy.

We believed that it was fine to conduct an autopsy and then immediately perform a medical exam on another person. Then we realized that washing our hands prevented severe infections.

We believed that it was okay to dump sewage into our drinking water sources. Then we discovered this was a source of deadly diseases.

It's easy to look back at our ancestors and laugh at them for their foolishness. Hopefully, one day our descendants will look back at our Old Happy beliefs and laugh at us, too.

Once you let go of society's definition,
you will be able to find happiness.

Luckily, we have a mechanism for correcting mistaken beliefs: our internal desire to learn more and more. There are always brave people who are exploring and pushing the boundaries of what we think we know. Thousands of scientists, philosophers, artists, activists, innovators, and people like you push us to shift our assumptions and explore new possibilities.

Just like we learned from germ theory that, yes, it's a good idea to wash your hands before examining patients, we now have gathered enough evidence to prove why Old Happy is so disastrously dangerous for our happiness. We can use this knowledge to drive a cultural transformation and create a happier world.

It's time for you to be happy. You've worked hard enough. You've conformed for long enough. You've waited long enough. It's time for you to find joy that lasts.

KEY TAKEAWAYS

- Everyone wants to be happy. The pursuit of happiness drives everything we do.

- To pursue happiness, we have to define it. We tend to unconsciously adopt society's definition of happiness for ourselves.

- Society tells us that happiness comes from achievement, perfection, and material gain; however, research shows that these pursuits do not make us happy.

- You have the power to change your definition of happiness.

2

The Hidden Forces That Shape Our Lives

To leave behind Old Happy and find true and lasting happiness, we need to start at the very beginning.

About three hundred eighty-five thousand babies are born every day. Each arrives in possession of that pure, beautiful desire for happiness that we all share. A newborn's definition of happiness is as narrow as it is universal: they will be happy if they are safe, get enough food and sleep, and experience love.

Now, let's jump to the present moment. Those babies have grown into adults who believe that they need to achieve specific goals in their career, be better than their neighbors, and make themselves as close to perfect as possible. They try very hard to do those things—often at the expense of their health, relationships, community, and planet—but even if they are successful, it doesn't actually make them happy.

What on *earth* happened to these babies?

THE WORLD TELLS US WHAT TO VALUE

In a 2013 paper, a global team of researchers in cultural neuroscience mapped out how people are socialized into a set of beliefs like Old Happy. This process begins in the first days of your life, when you start to receive messages from the culture and society you were born into. Neuroscience research shows that our brains are *extremely* sensitive to these external messages.

Every society values specific things. What's important? Who is celebrated? What do we strive for? In Western countries, our values are shaped by three prominent forces: individualism, capitalism, and domination.

These are big concepts that at first might seem so disconnected from you and your daily life. In fact, they have an enormous influence on you and your happiness.

Individualism

It's an important, wonderful thing to be your own person. Having freedom, goals, hopes, autonomy, and self-respect is essential for happiness.

This is the great strength of individualism, which was famously described by Alexis de Tocqueville, a French noble who visited America in 1835. He wrote about how Americans pursued freedom from oppression, celebrated individuality, and recognized human dignity. (Of course, these did not extend to all of the country's citizens.)

But individualism also has a downside. It teaches us that we are separate from other people. In de Tocqueville's words, individualism "disposes each member of the community to sever himself from the mass of his fellow-creatures."

In the United States, individualism is one of our strongest cultural values, and it continues to rise both here and in other countries. There are clever ways to measure this, like looking at the products that a culture creates. Psychologist Patricia Greenfield conducted a study of more than one and a half million books, starting with those published in 1800 and going all the way up to 2000. She found that, over time, individualistic words like *me*, *self*, and *unique* began to appear far more frequently, reflecting our shifting values. The word *get* quadrupled in use during the course of two hundred years. Another study looked at television shows made for tweens and calculated how often they celebrated specific values. In 1967, personal fame ranked fifteenth

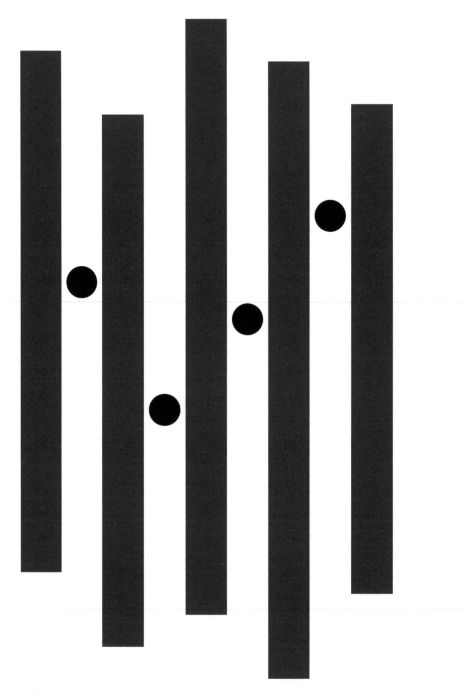

Individualism tells you that you are separate and better off alone.

out of sixteen of the top values. In 2007, it ranked first out of sixteen.

The second, more problematic outcome of individualism places the self at the center of absolutely everything. In fact, de Tocqueville himself worried this might happen, concerned that America's strength would turn into its weakness. Individualism emphasizes self-interest, even if it hurts others or the greater good. It teaches that your desires are more important than others' needs. It disconnects you from your communities. It tells you that you are on your own.

Individualism even influences the way that we conceptualize happiness: it's *my* happiness, not ours. It's this harmful aspect of individualism that underpins Old Happy.

Capitalism

In the same year that America was founded, the Scottish moral philosopher Adam Smith was writing about the economy—the same writing that would later make him known as the founding father of capitalism. He argued that individuals are rational and self-interested, and that if they pursue their self-interests, the needs of society will be simultaneously satisfied.

Capitalism is an economic system in which a small group of people control the means of production and a large group of people are responsible for doing the producing. Like individualism, capitalism has its strengths. Mohandas Gandhi, leader of India's independence campaign, once wrote that "capital as such is not evil; it is its wrong use that is evil." In its right use, capitalism has brought about advances in quality of life for many people. It has given the world new products, innovations, and experiences.

Capitalism's wrong use, though, has led to extraordinary inequality. It encourages endless consumerism. It turned economic value into the supreme societal metric of success and human worth. It built a rigged system that privileges the few but tells the many that they, too, can achieve financial security through hard work. It has resulted in a profound lack of social institutions that serve our communities, a vi-

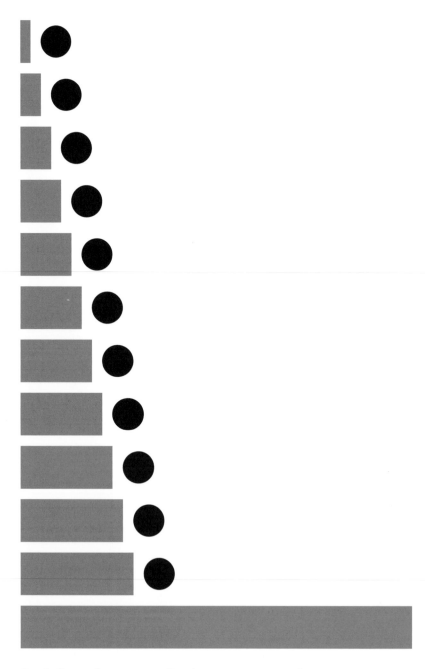

Capitalism tells you to endlessly pursue more and more.

cious gutting of our planet's resources, and the deprioritization of compassion in daily life in favor of ever-more growth.

Although Smith himself argued that there was a natural limit to human self-interest, it doesn't seem like we have found that limit yet. Capitalism gets us stuck on a hamster wheel, exerting so much effort just to spin around and around a hollow center. It powers the belief that working more, getting more, and having more will make us happy.

In her book *Becoming Wise*, journalist Krista Tippett beautifully illustrated this point, when she wrote:

> The paradise is here. Paradise is right in front of us. In capitalism what is engineered is longing, engineered longing and desire in us for what can be in the future. It's always about the next product, the next big thing . . . Come on. What if we actually were content with our lives? What if we actually knew this was paradise? It would be very hard to control us.

Domination

Finally, Old Happy is defined by the ways in which people dominate one another in pursuit of their individual happiness. We're clambering on one another to get to the top of the pile, not caring that we're stepping on people's bodies along the way.

The scholar bell hooks wrote in her book *Feminism is for Everybody* that "cultures of domination attack self-esteem, replacing it with a notion that we derive our sense of being from dominion over another." Instead of learning to value our unique selves, we are taught to value ourselves in comparison to others.

In a culture of domination, someone's humanity is ignored so that someone else can achieve their individualist, capitalist goals of pleasure, power, possessions, or popularity. In these situations, the pursuit of happiness is not simply misguided—it is actively hurting others. Recent studies have found that when people believe that life is an "I win, you lose" game, they are much more likely to treat others

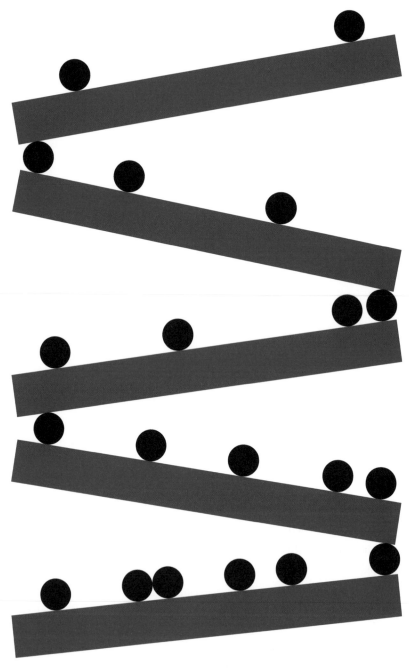

Domination tells you that you must oppress
other people to get what you want.

with aggression and intimidation. Other studies have found that the more hierarchical an environment is, the more people justify that it's okay to do harmful things to others.

In the early 1900s, Mohandas Gandhi established a pen-pal friendship with Leo Tolstoy, author of *War and Peace* and widely recognized as one of the greatest writers of all time. In later years, Gandhi was known to quote something that Tolstoy wrote to him: "if we would but get off the backs of our neighbours, the world would be quite all right." Domination is about climbing on someone else's back because you think it will make you happy.

This happens at a societal level, in the ways that we cast one group of people above another. Domination falsely says that there is a right way to be and a wrong way to be, and that those who are different should be punished. This includes racism, anti-Semitism, patriarchy and sexism, classism, ableism, heterosexism, genderism, and ageism. People who are not a part of the dominant group are treated unequally and unjustly, both in individual interactions and through the broader societal conditions that they must engage with every day.

From daily experiences of oppression to the ways that systems exploit, domination hurts billions of people. It teaches you that life is a competition, that people can be used to further your own aims, and that there is only value in one narrow way of being.

THESE VALUES INFORM OUR BEHAVIOR

Individualism, capitalism, and domination shape us all by telling us what is valuable. These values are then infused into and disseminated by the institutions, systems, media, and products that we grow up and live with, creating an Old Happy culture.

Think about it. How many times, through the years, have you heard these kinds of messages?

Individualism:
- You don't need other people.

- Figure it out by yourself.
- Do whatever you want.

Capitalism:
- You must be successful.
- You can't stop and rest.
- Your value is based on what you do.

Domination:
- You need to compete and win.
- Some people are better than others.
- You're never good enough.

The three forces all build upon and amplify one another, too. They're like the mythical three-headed Hydra monster, snapping at you to isolate yourself, work harder and harder, and prove your worth. So you do: you learn to behave in the ways that are celebrated and rewarded by Old Happy culture.

For example, consider how this culture has shaped the way that people typically behave on social media. We post about ourselves—individualism. We highlight our accomplishments and possessions—capitalism. And we strive to prove how exceptional we are and how much better we are than other people, in order to amass the greatest number of followers that we can—domination. Engaging in these behaviors can even perpetuate Old Happy culture further, sending other people those very same messages that hurt us.

OUR BEHAVIOR CHANGES OUR BELIEFS

Growing up and participating in Old Happy culture changes the way that you see the world. It creates what is known as a worldview.

A worldview is a set of beliefs and assumptions that shapes your life in profound ways. It's your personal model of the world, a version of reality you construct over the years based on your experiences. We use it to understand and explain the world around us, and in turn, it influences our behaviors.

None of us are consciously writing out our worldview and thoughtfully revising it as we grow up. This belief formation is happening at another, deeper level, as we engage in the world, learn from our experiences, and connect with other people.

When you're young, you use trial and error to learn the rules of the physical world: you can't walk through walls, stoves are hot, dropped objects fall to the floor (and sometimes smash into pieces). As you get older, you don't question it: use the door, don't touch the stove, be careful not to drop that glass. The same is true with the nonphysical world. You learn, from experience, that your problems must be solved by you alone, achievement leads to praise, and self-esteem is based on superiority. And you don't question it.

Once our worldview is formed, we have a tendency to live by it unquestioningly, believing that it is the whole truth and nothing but the truth. The author David Foster Wallace told a story in a 2005 commencement speech that illustrates its power:

> There are these two young fish swimming along and they happen to meet an older fish swimming the other way, who nods at them and says "Morning, boys. How's the water?" And the two young fish swim on for a bit, and then eventually one of them looks over at the other and goes, "What the hell is water?"

Our worldview is the water we are swimming in. And just like the younger fish, we have no idea that it exists. That gives it power over us. It's not the only factor that drives us, but it is one that has been largely unacknowledged in the way we talk about happiness. Things that are unacknowledged are extraordinarily hard to change, as the psychologist Carl Jung said: "The psychological rule says that when an inner situation is not made conscious, it happens outside as fate."

One way to think about your worldview is as your own personal search engine. It has been unconsciously filled with answers to so many questions, all the way from your belief about the universe ("Is there a God?"), to how you view other people ("Can people be trusted?"), to the meaning of life ("Is this all a simulation?").

Of the many possible questions in your worldview, there are three that matter the most for your happiness.

You have been pondering these three questions for your whole life. Slowly but surely, you have formed an answer, shaped by those billions of external, values-laden messages you have received from Old Happy culture.

They are the three most important questions you will ever ask yourself.

1. Who am I? This question is about your identity and how you see yourself.
2. What should I do? This question is about your goals, choices, and daily activities.
3. How am I related to others? This question is about your relationships with others and the greater world.

Although they might seem simple, these questions are the cornerstone of this book, of your personal happiness, and even—dare I say it—of the future well-being of humanity and survival of our planet. The three questions live at the heart of a human being's life, and since we were babies, Old Happy culture has taught us to answer these questions in a very specific way:

1. Who am I? I am lacking something.
2. What should I do? I must achieve expected outcomes.
3. How am I related to others? I am separate from others.

These answers tell you what you need to do in order to be happy. They make you believe: "I need to prove that I'm good enough. I will do it by achieving more and more. I will do it all by myself. *Then* I will be happy."

That is how those babies ended up here.

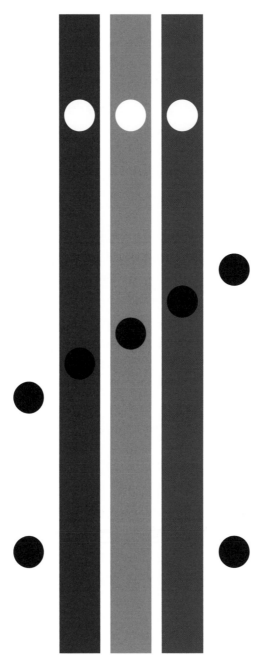

Old Happy makes you believe that you are lacking, you must
always achieve more, and you are on your own.

HOW OLD HAPPY HURTS US

A few years ago, scientists identified a strange phenomenon: it seemed that Americans who were aggressively pursuing happiness ended up unhappier than ever. What was going on?

It turns out that it was the way that they *defined* happiness that was leading to their increased depression, anxiety, and dissatisfaction. They had an Old Happy worldview. They had been led to believe that happiness would come from focusing more and more on the self, rather than on nurturing their relationships with others and using their gifts to help them.

This is exactly what happened to me. For the longest time, I thought that *I* was broken. I eventually learned that wasn't true. It was my compass that was broken—my worldview had been fundamentally disrupted, and it was leading me astray.

In real life, when compasses are exposed to powerful magnetic fields, the compass's needle can become depolarized and point in the opposite direction. Scientists have even discovered that if you put a magnet on a bird's head, that new magnetic force disrupts the bird's ability to navigate its migratory routes.

That magnetic force is what we're taught about happiness. It inevitably sends us, like those birds in the study, flying in the wrong direction. For no matter how loudly or frequently these societal forces proclaim it, there is no lasting joy to be found in isolation, acquisition, or superiority.

Old Happy reminds me a bit of a story I heard from a friend of mine named James. Every Christmas when he was a kid, his mom would make a special pudding. His favorite. One year, he tiptoed into the kitchen to sneak a bite before dinner. Opening the fridge door, he spotted a bowl on a high shelf covered with a dishcloth. He stretched his arm up and slid a spoon beneath the cloth, digging in to scoop up a giant bite. Suddenly, he heard footsteps approaching the kitchen. Not wanting to get caught, he shoved the full spoon into his mouth. But it wasn't pudding. It was lard.

That's what Old Happy is like: expecting a delicious dessert and getting a disgusting, greasy, tasteless blob of lard instead.

Haven't we all had this experience? Haven't we all felt the hollowness of this life we've decided that we're okay with, even though it's hurting us, our communities, and the planet? Aren't we *tired* of living this way?

FIND FREEDOM FROM OLD HAPPY

One of the barriers to eliminating Old Happy has been that we haven't had a name for it. Now, we do.

I hear it every single day: people feel a profound sense of confusion, sadness, and helplessness about the way that we are living. But without the language to describe it, it's just our normal.

In that gap, it's easy to jump to a default assumption: "There's something wrong with me." Old Happy wants you to think that! That belief will compel you to strive harder to conform, achieve, and isolate.

There is nothing wrong with you. What's wrong is our shared definition of happiness and how it is reinforced in our culture.

The philosopher Ludwig Wittgenstein wrote, "The limits of my language are the limits of my world." Just like the older fish shook the worlds of the younger fish by introducing the word *water*, we can shake our own worlds by naming the Old Happy worldview that we have taken for granted as the truth.

Here's how you do it: when you see an example of Old Happy, say, "Wow, that's so Old Happy."

- When you look in the mirror and hear that voice in your head criticizing your appearance, say: "That's Old Happy's voice, not mine."
- When you feel pressure to work more and more, say: "That's Old Happy trying to control me."
- When you feel that you can't ask for help, say: "That's Old Happy, lying to me that I'm all on my own."

- When you scroll social media and see people boasting about their cars and handbags, say: "I feel for them. They must be feeling pretty trapped by Old Happy."
- When you see a professor or a manager celebrating the person working the latest nights, say: "They're encouraging Old Happy behaviors."
- When you see a government implementing a policy that dominates others, say: "That is contributing to Old Happy culture."

Use the name to realize that *you* are not Old Happy. You are someone who *has been affected* by Old Happy. This will make it so much easier for you to accept and love yourself, pursue what matters to you, and build meaningful relationships with other people.

Just because we grew up with this worldview doesn't mean we need to live with it for the rest of our lives. Starting today, you can name Old Happy for what it is, and in the process, begin to free yourself from it.

KEY TAKEAWAYS

- Our society teaches us what to value. We create a culture that promotes these values. In living in that culture, we build a worldview, or our mental model of the world.

- Within your worldview, three key questions matter the most for your happiness: Who am I? What should I do? How am I related to others?

- Old Happy teaches you that you are lacking something, that you need to achieve expected outcomes, and that you are separate from others.

- You have the power to free yourself from Old Happy. Start naming it when you see it, and you will create the space for real happiness.

3

How to Start Building
a Happy Life

In the early 1950s, Fred Rogers, a college student studying music, turned on his parents' brand-new television for the first time.

He absolutely hated what he saw.

The children's programs were frantic and overwhelming, full of costumed characters throwing pies at one another and punctuated by advertisements that promised happiness that could be purchased.

He wondered: What if he could create a different type of television show, one that actually helped kids feel good and do good?

Seventeen years later, his own television show premiered: *Mister Rogers' Neighborhood*. At the beginning of every episode, he would walk into his on-set house, take off his suit jacket and zip up his iconic cardigan, swap his dress shoes for sneakers, and then talk to children like they mattered.

For thirty-one seasons, he was there for kids.

He was there during the Cold War, using puppets to explain why it's so dangerous to stockpile weapons.

He was there after the *Challenger* space shuttle disaster, devoting a week of episodes to talking about death and the pain of grief.

He was there for kids who felt unloved and lonely, there for kids whose parents were getting divorced, there for kids who were being left out at school, there for kids who had made a mistake, and there for kids who were experiencing all of the ups and downs of being a kid.

Because he was there, he became one of the most beloved figures in the United States. At one point in time, he received more mail than anyone else in the country—and he responded to every single letter. His red knit cardigan is in the Smithsonian. His legacy included Emmys, a Peabody Award, the Presidential Medal of Freedom, a U.S. postage stamp, an asteroid named after him, a star on the Hollywood Walk of Fame, and a celebratory Google Doodle. But most importantly, he taught generations of children to be kind to themselves and to others.

No one ever would have predicted that a shy, lonely boy who just wanted to make music would grow up and become one of the most iconic figures of all time, someone who made a tremendous difference in the world while also experiencing lasting happiness.

How did he do it? Rogers discovered the rules for a happy life—the two same threads that I traced in my research—that you'll be learning about in this book:

1. Discover who you really are.
2. Use it to help other people.

Test these rules for yourself. Think about the happiest people you know. You'll probably see that they know who they are and are finding ways to help those around them. Or think about the people you admire the most. What are they doing? Sharing their unique gifts with the world, trying to make it a better place.

These rules helped Rogers create a life of purpose and joy, a life that provided him with "a sense of wholeness."

WHY YOU NEED TO BE YOURSELF

Rogers was three years old when he demonstrated a talent for music. Before the age of five, he was playing full songs on the piano. Despite being a musical prodigy, he didn't have an easy childhood. He was

There are two rules for a happy life: discover who you are
and use your gifts to help other people.

frequently ill, forced to spend many hours alone in his room. It was there that he began to tell stories and make up songs, imagining the make-believe world that would one day populate his television show. He described his childhood as lonely, recalling that every time he was alone, he would start to cry. He was bullied and didn't have any real friends. Luckily, as he grew older, he began to find the people around him who loved and appreciated him for who he was.

From these unique experiences, Rogers developed specific gifts, like a talent for music, a capacity for empathy, and the awareness of how difficult a childhood can be.

You, too, have your own unique gifts. They're the things that make you *you*. Your gifts aren't just about the things you can do. They're also about what you have been through, what you have learned, and the person you are, deep down.

In a commencement speech, Rogers told a story about sitting in on a class taught by Yo-Yo Ma, the acclaimed cellist. One of the young students finished playing Brahms' Cello Sonata. In response, Yo-Yo said, "Nobody else can make the sound you make."

There's only one Mister Rogers. And there's only one you.

SHARE YOURSELF WITH THE WORLD

At Rollins College, where Rogers got his undergraduate degree, there's a walkway between buildings where a small plaque is displayed. Engraved in marble, it says: *Life Is for Service*. Rogers wrote down that motto and carried it in his wallet for the rest of his life.

Rogers saw his television show as an act of service. In 1969, President Richard Nixon was trying to cut funding for children's educational programs. Rogers went to Congress to expertly argue to keep the twenty million dollars of funding in the budget and gave a short speech we can all learn from, describing his acts of service:

> I give an expression of care every day to each child, to help him realize that he is unique. I end the program by saying,

"You've made this day a special day, by just your being you. There's no person in the whole world like you, and I like you, just the way you are." And I feel that if we in public television can only make it clear that feelings are mentionable and manageable, we will have done a great service for mental health.

In response, the chairman of the Senate Subcommittee on Communications, said, "I'm supposed to be a pretty tough guy, and this is the first time I've had goosebumps in the past two days. I think it's wonderful. Looks like you just earned yourself twenty million dollars."

Looking at Rogers's life, it's easy to put him on a pedestal. That's *Mister Rogers*! He's not like the rest of us. But in an interview after his death in 2003, his wife of fifty years, Joanne, warned of the dangers of thinking this way. She says she hears it all the time: "I would love to be like him, but I can't." She was resolute that, no, anyone can be like Mister Rogers.

She didn't mean that anyone could have a heartfelt television show with puppets, songs, and stories. She meant that anyone could take the same path that Rogers did: discovering who they are and using it to help other people. Your life shouldn't look like his, because that wouldn't reflect *you*! You need to discover your own unique way to serve, whether it's with your family and friends, in your community, through your work, or even in the broader world.

YOUR HAPPINESS CAN CHANGE THE WORLD

This journey you're going on isn't only going to benefit you. It's going to impact so many other people around you.

Our world *doesn't* have to be like this. The systems and beliefs at the core of Old Happy are made up. Over time, a group of people have decided that these are worth perpetuating, enforcing, and defending. That's why they stick around.

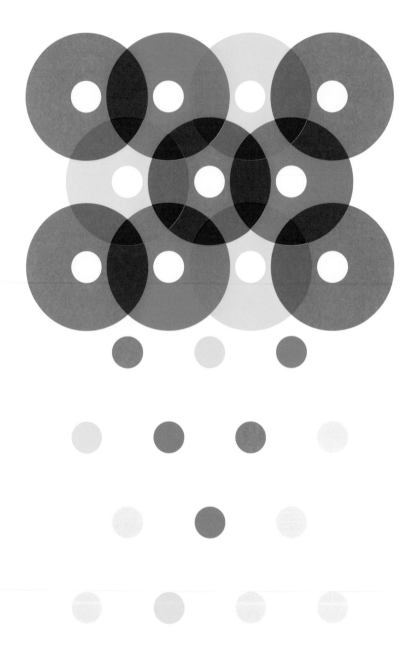

As you discover and share your gifts, you will be
helping other people find happiness, too.

Millions of people have rejected the false promises of Old Happy— like Fred Rogers, who said, "The older I get, the more I come to understand that the things we possess can never bring us ultimate happiness." People like him are everywhere, working to change and improve conditions. You can join them.

One study found that it only takes 25 percent of the population to create a tipping-point effect that drives massive social change. Sometimes, all it takes is a single person to join in an effort that ends up tipping the scales in the right direction and ushering in a broader change. In a recent poll, only 12 percent of Americans said they were "very happy"—the lowest percentage ever recorded since the poll began in 1972. This is distressing. But it's also an opportunity for us to, once and for all, remake our world into a happier one.

You don't need to quit your job, change your entire life, start a nonprofit, or create a business to change the world. All it takes is one different choice: the choice to pursue happiness in a new way.

Rogers had no way of knowing, when he turned on that television set for the first time, where his life would take him. He simply chose then, and again and again, to be himself and give of himself, which led to more and more joy for himself and others.

At any moment, you, too, can make a different choice, and that choice can change your life *and* the world, at the same time. Today could be the day that you look back at years from now and think, "That choice changed everything for me." Other people out there also will be thinking, "Their choice changed everything for me, too."

If enough of us can shift our definition of happiness, we can also shift our world, creating a place where everyone is valued for who they are, everyone has the chance to contribute, and everyone gets what they need. A New Happy world.

THE FOUR STEPS TO HAPPINESS

In the following pages, we are going to go on a journey that helps you find happiness. This journey has four steps.

First, we need to transform your worldview, from an Old Happy one to a New Happy one. Right now, you are carrying the incredibly heavy, burdensome weight of Old Happy around with you, all day, every day. It's like you have been running an endless uphill marathon, while wearing a weighted vest, without even knowing it. Through this first step, you're going to get to remove the weight from your exhausted shoulders. You'll learn: you are enough, you can pursue what matters to you, and you are connected to other people. I can't wait for you to see how free you will feel—and how much self-love, joy, and purpose you will get to experience because of it.

Once we have rewired your worldview, you'll be ready to learn the surprising secret to happiness, the very best way to put the rules of being yourself and giving yourself into action.

Then, you'll discover your gifts—the things that make you *you*. There are three types of gifts, and you possess each kind. You will learn how to tap into them and start using them in your daily life.

Finally, we'll bring it all together and explore how to share your gifts with others, building a life around them through your work, in your community, and in the world.

Are you ready to find happiness and change the world at the same time?

KEY TAKEAWAYS

- Happiness comes from discovering who you are and sharing yourself in ways that help other people.

- You don't need to change your whole life. Happiness starts with just one different choice.

- This choice won't just benefit you, but will benefit the world around you.

PART TWO

Unwind Old Happy

4

The First Lie: You're Not Enough

It's the late 1990s, and Demi Moore is the most celebrated movie star of her generation. The public swoons over her beauty, her work, and her life. She just became the highest-paid actress in Hollywood history, and she's married to an action hero. From the outside, it seems that her life is perfect.

Twenty years later, she looked back and shared what that time was really like: her marriage was falling apart, she experienced body image issues, and she spent her days in a constant state of self-doubt and insecurity. As she wrote in her autobiography, "No matter what success I had, I just never felt good enough."

We hear it time and again from those who hit every milestone of "success" that Old Happy sets for us: no matter what you do, you're never enough.

David Bowie admitted, in an interview with Q Magazine, that he experienced self image problems and very low self esteem which left him feeling inadequate. As a result he hid behind his writing and performing, believing his value was in how good his music could be.

Julie Andrews hid her Academy Award for her performance in *Mary Poppins* in her attic because she feared she didn't deserve it.

One study of 116 CEOs and executives identified that they had one fear in common: they were not good enough to have gotten their jobs.

These stories point us to an important truth. No amount of external rewards, success, or validation can help you feel good enough. Worldwide fame and acclaim, Academy Awards, and prestigious job titles don't give it to you. You will never find your sense of "enough" by striving to meet Old Happy's standards—it simply isn't possible. It's like gambling at a casino: the house always wins.

Why is it that, despite everything you do, it feels like you're still not good enough? Because at the core of the Old Happy worldview is the message that no matter how hard you try, you are always lacking something. Deep down, you're flawed, broken, and *bad*.

THE LACK LIE

The first worldview question is: Who am I?

Old Happy's answer: You are lacking something.

Every week, I host a virtual check-in for the New Happy community, during which people share what they need help with. After years of these weekly check-ins, and reading tens of thousands of messages, I have learned a lot about what people struggle with.

There is one thing that appears in these check-ins, again and again and again:

"I'm not good enough."

"When will I feel worthy?"

"I feel like there's something wrong with me."

Perhaps you have wondered, "Am I the only one who feels like I'm not good enough?" I promise you, you are not alone. In fact, this belief that we're lacking seems to be one that we all share.

It's also a belief that compels us to treat ourselves terribly. We have been taught by Old Happy to hate ourselves for our humanity and to punish ourselves accordingly. While self-hatred might sound dramatic,

The first lie: no matter what you do and no matter
how hard you try, you are always lacking.

how often do you treat yourself like an enemy or an adversary? Look through your own self-talk for the evidence. It likely sounds something like this:

"You idiot."

"What's wrong with you?"

"You never do anything right!"

"If only you were different . . ."

This voice in your head—the one that keeps telling you that you are not good enough—that's not really you. It's the result of growing up in a culture that told you that no matter what you do, you are not enough. That's why unwinding Old Happy starts with learning a new way to relate to yourself—with unconditional self-acceptance, knowing that you are worthy exactly as you are.

WHY WE GRADE OURSELVES AND HOW TO STOP

Old Happy has convinced you that your worth is based not just on your performance, but on constantly achieving more and more. It also has convinced you to perpetuate this idea by grading yourself constantly in your progress toward this inhumane goal.

Have you ever noticed how often you do this?

"That was a mediocre presentation."

"I'd give myself a C on that project."

"At least I did better than Jake did."

Grading ourselves against an external standard is a behavior that Old Happy socialized us into a long time ago. Along the way, we also learned to use that grading system to define our value as people.

We rate ourselves and then we use that rating to judge whether we are good or bad. (Spoiler alert: we're always bad.) These leaps happen really quickly. It may sound like this:

> *"I forgot Bryan's birthday—I'm such a bad person."*

> *"I can't believe I snapped at Sarah—I'm a terrible parent."*

> *"I should have caught the mistake in the report—I knew I wasn't good enough for this job."*

Your performance does not have anything to do with your worth. The two are unrelated. Every time you grade yourself, you are reinforcing Old Happy, sending yourself the message that you are not doing enough, you do not have enough, you are not good enough.

The next time you catch yourself beating yourself up, try this tool. I call it "the Breakup," and it helps you disconnect your performance from your self-worth.

Take the following thought:

> *"I forgot Bryan's birthday—I'm such a bad person."*

Next, break it up into two sentences:

> *"I forgot Bryan's birthday. I'm such a bad person."*

The first sentence is a fact. The second is an Old Happy lie.

Drop the second sentence, and replace it with a recognition that you are still worthy, no matter what you do:

> *"I forgot Bryan's birthday. I'm still worthy as a person."*

This method was proposed in the 1950s by psychologist Albert Ellis, who invented the first form of cognitive behavioral therapy. He argued that using one event or behavior to evaluate your entire self-worth is not only completely illogical, but also the source of our suffering. His solution: unconditional self-acceptance. Accept yourself no matter what, even if you wish you had done better or behaved differently.

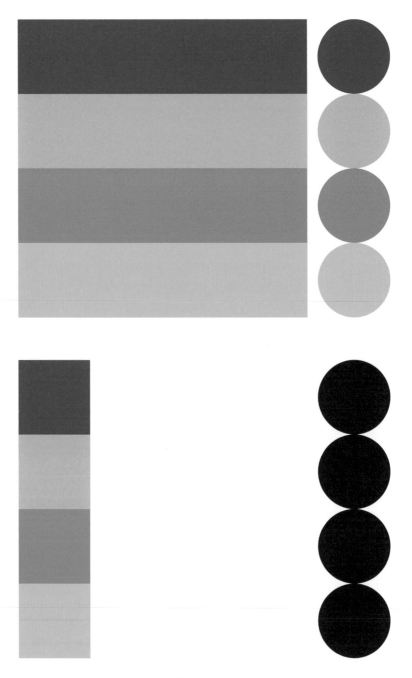

What you do does not define who you are. Separate the two.
You are always worthy, no matter what you do.

Here are a few other ways you can use this approach:

"I made a mistake on that report. I know my worth isn't based upon my performance."

"I hurt Melissa with that comment. I recognize I'm a good person who made a mistake."

"I couldn't get everything done today. I tried my best, though."

You might be thinking, "Is this just letting myself off the hook?" In fact, it's the opposite.

When you haven't done the Breakup, a mistake or a struggle can feel extremely threatening to your sense of self because it feels like the mistake dictates your self-worth. Think back to a time when you felt that your self-worth was on the line. How did you behave? I know my impulse: feel defensive, lash out, judge. Trying to prove that we are good enough usually turns into trying to prove how superior we are.

On the other hand, when you accept yourself no matter what happens, it helps quiet this impulse. In one study, participants were asked to record a video introducing themselves. A researcher then gave either positive or negative feedback about the video. People who were more accepting of and compassionate toward themselves were far less defensive than those who weren't.

When you're secure in your worth, it's so much easier to see the moments where you need to change, apologize, and learn. You know that it's only one event and that it doesn't define who you are as a person.

"I made a mistake on that report. Looking back, I see that I was moving too quickly and felt rushed. The next time I have to send a report, I'm going to start the night before."

"I hurt Melissa with that comment. I wasn't thinking about how my words might have been interpreted. Next time, I want to remember to pause before I speak."

"I couldn't get everything done today. Maybe there's too much on my plate. Would it help me to deprioritize some things? Could I ask someone at work to take that project?"

This approach even makes you more persistent and, therefore, more likely to achieve your goals. One study asked undergraduates to take two difficult vocabulary tests. On the first try, most of them failed. Afterward, some of them were shown a message reminding them to be kind to themselves. Then they all were given a chance to study for the second test. Those who got the self-compassion reminder studied for longer than those who didn't.

You can stop beating yourself up and entrenching your self-hatred and instead choose a new response—one in which the evaluation of your self-worth is off the table but responsibility for your behaviors is not.

Every day, there are moments when you judge yourself. With the Breakup tool, you can turn them into moments of kindness instead. Making these small shifts might not seem like it can change much. But with a bit of practice, self-acceptance will become your default response.

These grades, though, bring up an important question. Where exactly are they coming from?

THE TYRANNY OF THE PERFECT SELF

I remember a day, ten or so years ago, when I was beating myself up for making a mistake at work. I sat there, smacking my head into my hands, saying, "God, why are you such an idiot?" and "You are the worst!"

Suddenly, I had a flash of insight: who was I grading myself against?

I wasn't comparing myself to someone else, like a friend or a role model. I wasn't comparing myself to my past self. My reference for comparison was a perfect version of me who existed only in my head. This is something I call the perfect self.

The endless expectations of the perfect self keep you trapped.

This realization shook my world. I had never realized this criterion existed, that I was using it to grade myself, and how outrageously unrealistic my expectations for myself were.

In school, where we learned how to grade and judge ourselves, there was a rubric or an objective score or a letter grade. In life, we develop our own rubric: this perfect self.

The perfect self comes from Old Happy culture. Individualism says the perfect self is always strong and independent, handles everything by itself, and never feels difficult emotions.

Capitalism tells us the perfect self is successful, contributing to the economy, following the "right" path in the "right way," and, of course, is always productive. We're sold a million products and services promising a solution to our imperfect existence, and when they don't work, we blame ourselves for it.

Dominance establishes the "right" way to be. Writer and philosopher Audre Lorde called this the "mythical norm" of being white, cisgender, male, young, heterosexual, able-bodied, and Christian. This ideal is used to set a standard for normal. If you do not embody these characteristics, you're dehumanized for simply being who you are. This is reinforced through interactions with the world because our society is built *by* the mythical norm *for* the mythical norm. Even the "pursuit of happiness" enshrined in America's Declaration of Independence was only intended to apply to a certain subset of people.

Finally, we bring our own personal experiences into the mix: what our families, relationships, communities, and cultures tell us we should be. As one of the leading perfectionism researchers, Simon Sherry, once said, "It takes a village to raise a perfectionist."

The perfect self is the version of ourselves we think we need to become in order to be happy. It's a shadow silently moving next to us, reminding us of all of the ways that we are failing to measure up: others do it all, others do it perfectly, and others do it without breaking a sweat.

Imagine there was a job description that summarized the role of the perfect self.

HELP WANTED

In this role, it will be your job to do the following:

- Hide who you are and conform to a norm.
- Please every person you meet.
- Achieve world-changing impact by the age of twenty-one.
- Be beautiful/handsome. (Note: the ideal hire must be willing to change their appearance as soon as societal beauty standards change.)
- Never stumble, stress, or struggle.

Hours: 24/7/365.

Pay: none.

Performance measured on a minute-by-minute basis with real-time feedback offered via an implant in your brain.

Apply within!

Would you apply for this job? I don't think so. If you got it, how long do you think you would last? How would it affect your well-being?

Take a few moments and bring to mind your own perfect self:

- What do they do every day?
- What do they look like?
- What do they own?
- What have they achieved?
- What are their relationships like?

The clearer your mental picture of your perfect self is, the easier it will be to recognize its presence.

Intellectually, we know this perfect self is unattainable. But really knowing that in our bones is different. Deep down, I think a lot of us believe that if we push ourselves more and try a little bit harder and please just one other person, we'll claw our way to perfection and maybe even find a way to stay there.

It's a tantalizing prospect. Some days, you might feel like you're close to being your perfect self. It feels so good. You've finally figured out life. And then the next day, when you mess up or stumble, you beat yourself up and resolve to push yourself even harder.

This is where our self-hatred comes from. Because it seems like the only thing standing between you and your perfect self is *you*: if you could just work a little harder, be more organized, master that productivity technique, build better habits, suppress your feelings, or stop being so difficult or sensitive or emotional or different or whatever, then you could become the perfect self, and you'd finally be happy.

HOW TO LET GO OF THE
PERFECT SELF

In 2022, Taylor Swift received an honorary doctorate from New York University and gave the commencement speech to graduates. She described how the way we grade ourselves constantly reinforces the poisonous idea of the perfect self. In the moving speech, Taylor spoke about her own experience of coming up in the music industry as a young adult. She told the graduates that she was made to feel that if she didn't make any mistakes and presented perfectly, all the children of America would grow up to be 'perfect angels'. She feared that if she did make a mistake and show her flaws then the 'entire earth would fall off its axis' and it would be all her fault. This perfectionism came from the fear that making mistakes and failing would take away any opportunity for a happy and fulfilling life.

She's right. Research shows perfectionism is strongly related to depression, social disconnection, and increased suicide risk. In a sample of young adults, researchers discovered that when perfectionists are under stress, their immune system becomes dysregulated, potentially explaining why they also have worse health outcomes and earlier mortality. One study of more than forty thousand college students found that the external pressure to be perfect increased by 33 percent between 1989 and 2016. Leading researchers have argued that one in three children now has a harmful form of perfectionism.

Our quest for the perfect self hurts other people, too. Those who are most trapped by it also demand perfection from others, promote conformity, or seek to dominate through being "superior." Parents can pass on their perfectionism to their kids; the more that parents respond to their children's mistakes with criticism and the higher their expectations for their kids, the more likely their children are to become perfectionists themselves.

The first step to releasing the perfect self is to learn how to notice its presence. There are certain places where it likes to assert itself:

- Life roles: "I have to be the perfect parent, child, employee . . ."
- Goals: "I can't start this project unless I know it will work out."
- School: "Anything less than straight A's means I am a failure."
- Work: "I must get promoted next year, or my career is over."
- Home: "The house has to be spotless before anyone comes over."
- Relationships: "I need to appear perfect to find someone who will love me."

Your emotions also will alert you to the presence of the perfect self. Pay attention when you feel stuck, overwhelmed, frustrated, or resentful. In these moments, ask yourself, "What is my perfect self telling me to do, say, get, or achieve right now?"

Here's an example from my own life. When I was writing this

book, I got a major case of writer's block. It lasted for weeks until I realized what was really going on:

- My perfect self would be able to write this book effortlessly, spitting out one perfect draft on my first attempt.
- I couldn't do that, obviously. Therefore, I became unacceptable.
- I graded myself accordingly: "I can't write this book—I'm unworthy."
- That led to more pain. I became much more stressed, snapped at my loved ones, and struggled to write any words at all.

Here's what to do when you notice your own perfect self:

- Acknowledge it: In a world that tells you perfection leads to happiness, your perfect self is a coping mechanism that is trying to protect you from suffering. In your head or out loud, say, "Perfect self, I know you're trying to help, but you're actually making things harder."
- Reclaim control: Tell it, "I don't need you to say these things because I now know I don't need to be perfect to be happy."

The more you do this, the quieter your perfect self will get, and the more peace you will experience.

Striving to be your perfect self is like being desperately thirsty in the desert. You have hallucinated a mirage and are stumbling toward what seems like an oasis, but no matter how far you walk, you never get any closer. It is an illusion that can never, ever be fulfilled.

MEET YOUR TRUE SELF

Don't just give up on your perfect self because it's a source of misery. Give up on it because it's blocking you from a source of joy: accepting and embracing your true self.

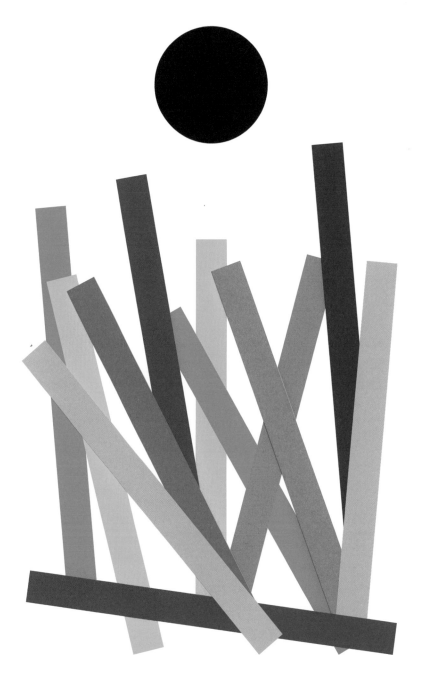

When you free yourself from the perfect self,
you can be who you really are.

Every single spiritual tradition has argued that, beneath all your Old Happy conditioning, there is a part of you that is loving, connected, and good, exactly as you are. This is your true self.

More recently, therapists and scientists have been investigating the true self. One compelling example comes from the work of Dr. Richard Schwartz, who created a revolutionary type of therapy called Internal Family Systems, which is grounded in this idea. During his forty years of practice, he has discovered that every single one of his clients has a true self. When people connect with this part of themselves, they can access all of the virtues we associate with goodness: wisdom, courage, kindness, acceptance, and love.

This is your true self. You are born with it. You can never lose it. You don't need to change who you are or achieve something to access it. You only need to clear what's in its way.

This is exactly what you are doing every time you let go of the perfect self. You're clearing the way for your true self to emerge.

This can be a radical idea, especially for those of us who have been taught we are bad. But you can connect with your true self directly and experience your own goodness for yourself. Here's one way to do it:

1. Think about a difficult experience you've had lately: a conflict, painful emotions, or an ongoing challenge.
2. Imagine you can connect with the part of you that's struggling.
3. Extend love to that part of you. That might be spoken words like, "I'm here for you," or "That was really hard." It could be breathing deeply, putting your hand on your heart, or imagining giving yourself a hug. If you're not sure what to do, imagine how you would treat a friend in this situation.

You will see that there are two parts of you: the first part that was in pain and the second part that was extending love. They're both *you*, but the second is your true self, the part of you that is always there to love, help, and connect. When you connect with your true self, the idea of not being "enough" becomes quaint and foolish. Look at you! You're absolutely wonderful.

YOU ARE ENOUGH

Many of us withhold love from ourselves, thinking that someday we'll finally embody the perfect self and then we will be worthy of our own love. Today is a day when you can choose to accept and love yourself exactly as you are.

We've been taught that *imperfect* means "bad." In reality, our imperfections make us human, and our humanity is what endows us with our true self, the source of our goodness. The two cannot be divorced. You are good and you are imperfect, and you always will be both. You have strengths and weaknesses; you have helped and you have hurt; you have succeeded and you have failed. You are a human being, imperfect and worthy just as you are, living alongside other human beings, all imperfect and worthy just as they are, too.

It's our quest to fulfill Old Happy's idea of good—perfection—that prevents us from accessing our own immutable inner goodness. The busier you are trying to be your perfect self, the less time you have to connect with your goodness and share it with others. This is the source of your gifts—something you'll learn a lot more about in later chapters.

Every day, you can make the choice to stop grading yourself, let go of your perfect self, and connect with your true self. As you do this, you're shifting into the New Happy worldview. You start to realize, "I really am enough, just as I am."

KEY TAKEAWAYS

- The first Old Happy lie is that you are lacking something.

- Use the Breakup tool to separate your self-worth from your actions. You can address your behavior without evaluating whether or not you're good enough.

- The perfect self is the version of ourselves we think we need to be in order to be happy. We measure ourselves against it constantly.

- When you notice your perfect self, acknowledge that it is trying to help you and then let it go.

- Letting go of your perfect self helps you connect with your true self—your good, loving, and connected nature.

5

The Second Lie:
You'll Be Happy When . . .

Andre Agassi is a tennis champion who won eight Grand Slams during his career. After he reached number one in his field, he said, "I felt nothing."

I felt nothing.

In my research, I spoke with a woman named Brandy, who told me about the culmination of her fifteen-year journey into academia. "I got a PhD, I got a tenure-track job at a top university, and then I got tenure. I felt nothing, really. Just a feeling of, 'I put myself through all that for this?'"

One of my friends spent eight years waiting to become a lawyer, only to discover it makes her miserable; now she's waiting for retirement. Another has burnt out three different times due to his job but remains certain that, when he gets promoted, *then* he'll finally be happy.

You also might be able to remember a time when you worked hard toward something, achieved it, and then felt surprised that the high so quickly faded away, leaving you feeling nothing—or worse, unhappy.

THE OUTCOME LIE

The second worldview question is: What should I do?

Old Happy's answer is: you must achieve expected outcomes.

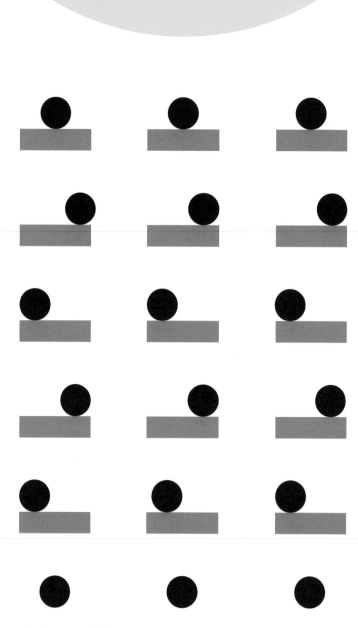

The second lie: once you get there, you will be happy.

You have an amazing capacity that you probably take for granted: your ability to set and pursue goals. You can imagine future possibilities for yourself, come up with a plan, and make it happen.

Why, then, do so many of us end up like Agassi and Brandy—pursuing goals with all of our incredible imagination and energy that then leave us feeling . . . nothing?

Nearly forty years ago, two psychologists, Richard Ryan and Edward Deci, met up to chat about goals. This conversation sparked a decades-long collaboration, hundreds of studies, and the establishment of "self-determination theory," one of the most important theories in psychology. With their collaborators Ken Sheldon and Tim Kasser, they have taught us a lot about how goals can help (or hinder) our happiness.

There are two types of goals: extrinsic and intrinsic.

Extrinsic goals are focused on gaining external approval and rewards. These are Old Happy outcomes, things we believe we have to do in order to be happy. Here are the most common ones:

- Popularity: to be admired by many people
- Conformity: to please others
- Image: to be beautiful
- Financial success: to be rich

These outcomes do not actually provide happiness in and of themselves. We pursue them because we think that having them will, in some way, lead to happiness.

It's not just *what* you're pursuing that matters; the *why* behind it is important, too. Often, you're pursuing the outcome because of Old Happy beliefs:

- You think you have to be the perfect self: "I must get accepted into this school to be worthy."
- You're competing with someone else for it: "This is what everyone else is doing."

- You'll be punished or rewarded for it: "If I don't do this, my parents will be angry with me."

For our whole lives, we've been internalizing instructions about what we need to do that come from the endless parade of successes we see online, the celebrations that are given for achieving them, and the consequences imposed if we break away from what's expected.

This is what happened to Agassi. He didn't choose to be a tennis player. His father chose for him. When he was a baby, his father, an Olympic boxer, declared that he would make his son into the greatest tennis player in the world. His dad built a tennis court in their backyard and created a machine that fired tennis balls that Agassi called "the dragon." He had to please the dragon by hitting twenty-five hundred balls a day. In his autobiography, you can feel his agony as he hits and hits and hits, yet no matter how hard he tries, it's never enough.

Tennis stardom was an Old Happy outcome, and because of that, Agassi never felt satisfied, no matter how many tournaments he won, no matter how much he was celebrated, and no matter how much money he earned. As he said, "I play tennis for a living even though I hate tennis, hate it with a dark and secret passion and always have."

Think back to goals you have pursued in the past.

Was this goal . . .

- Something that someone else (family, community, or culture) chose for you?
- Something you chose because another person had already achieved it?
- Something that would make you feel like you're "winning" in the competition of life?

Did you believe that, if you achieved that goal, it would . . .

- Prove you're good enough?

- Make all of your other problems disappear?
- Make it possible for you to finally relax or quit and do what really matters to you?

As you worked toward this goal, did you . . .

- Sacrifice other things (hobbies, relationships, health, or values) that are important to you?
- Feel pressured to achieve it within a specific time frame or in a certain way?
- Find yourself more and more unhappy without knowing why?

If you answered yes to any of these questions, you know what it's like to be under the sway of the Old Happy outcome.

WHY EXTRINSIC GOALS WON'T MAKE YOU HAPPY

It's normal to be tempted by extrinsic goals and what they seem to dangle in front of you. Recently, The New Happy's design work was in contention for an award. As I waited to hear the results, I would find myself thinking, "I hope we win!" On the heels of such hopeful thoughts, though, came the clinging, grasping ones, like "If I win this award, I will be so much happier," and "This award would prove my work is good enough."

Thoughts like, "I'll be happy when . . ." or "Once this happens . . ." are a cue that Old Happy is in your head. In these moments, you want to return to the power of labeling. Say to yourself, "That's Old Happy, not me." That's what I did: I texted a friend and told her how I was feeling, and it helped clear the fog.

As alluring as extrinsic goals may seem, they will never bring happiness. They can't—they don't satisfy our fundamental needs. In fact, extensive studies have found that extrinsic goals are more likely to be associated with unhappiness, including:

- Worse mental and physical health (including greater anxiety and depression)
- Lower life satisfaction
- Lower-quality relationships
- Less frequent positive emotions
- Less confidence
- More stress

And, in an ironic twist, studies have found that people who pursue extrinsic goals are less likely to achieve them.

Even if you *really* want to achieve that extrinsic goal, and you work *really* hard to succeed, it won't fulfill you. One 2014 study looked at two groups of lawyers. Those in the first group were pursuing the extrinsic goal of financial success through high-paying jobs. The second group focused on making a difference, taking lower-paying but meaningful jobs in nonprofits, sustainability, or public service. The lawyers in the second group were both happier and healthier, even though those in the first group were getting what they "wanted."

Pursuing these goals strengthens your Old Happy worldview, because it reinforces the idea that the world is a competition. Money, popularity, and status feel scarce, like things you have to fight for. You always need to work harder, push more, hustle better. Never take your eyes off the person next to you in case they grab a piece of your pie. Use your achievements to prove how much better you are compared to them. Of course, this mindset becomes a self-fulfilling prophecy that intensifies our culture of competition. This constant comparison is why studies show that extrinsic goals are also associated with less satisfying relationships.

To sum it all up: if you pursue outcomes, you're likely not going to be as happy pursuing them; you're less likely to achieve them; and, if you do manage to achieve them, they won't make you happy. What a terrible deal! It's like trying to fill a bucket that has a hole in it. No matter how many times you fill it, it just empties again.

When I look at outcomes, here's what I think about: the fact that we still pursue these goals with so much determination proves to me how deeply and truly we want to be happy. We're willing to endure a great deal of pain in the moment for something that we believe will make us happy in the future. It's dreadful that it doesn't actually work.

INTRINSIC GOALS BRING YOU JOY
ALONG THE WAY

Let's look at another tennis player, Roger Federer—winner of twenty Grand Slams, the third most of all time—whose path to the sport was quite different from Agassi's.

Federer loved playing sports as a kid, especially soccer and tennis. At age eleven, he decided he wanted to focus on tennis, mostly because he liked playing a solo sport more than a team one. It was his authentic choice to pursue his career, and the rest is sports history.

This is the second type of goal: an intrinsic goal. The key types of intrinsic goals are as follows:

- Safety: feeling secure and providing for yourself and loved ones
- Health: taking care of your well-being
- Self-acceptance: learning to love yourself
- Growth: finding ways to transform
- Connection: building positive relationships
- Community: being a part of a group and making a contribution to others

In stark contrast to extrinsic goals, research shows that intrinsic goals *do* make you happier. Pursuing these goals satisfies your innate needs, making them enjoyable, meaningful, and fulfilling—and not just at the end when you achieve your goal, but along the way, too.

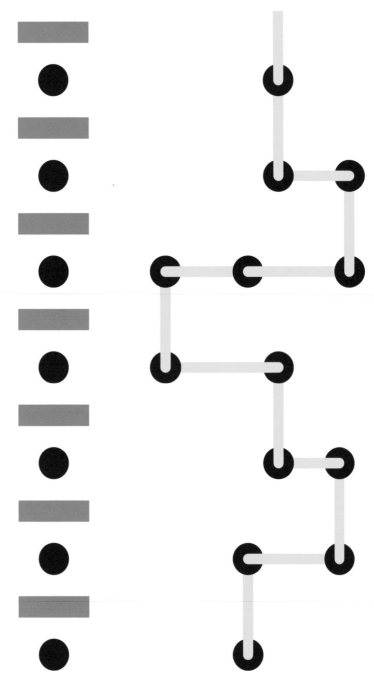

Intrinsic goals come from within and bring you joy along the way.

We've seen this play out for Federer. In a 2016 interview, he said, "I love tennis in such a big way that I don't care if I don't win so much anymore."

HOW TO TURN OFF OLD HAPPY AUTOPILOT

Autopilot systems are designed to let humans sit back while technology controls a vehicle's direction and speed. They're supposed to help free up the driver's attention so that they can focus on the more complex elements of the journey.

Old Happy has put us all on autopilot. It's navigating us toward extrinsic goals and controlling our speed: *faster, faster, faster.* We're just along for the ride, feeling that bewildered unhappiness that says, "I'm doing everything right! Why aren't I happy yet?"

Instead of helping us focus on the bigger picture, Old Happy autopilot has distracted us from it. When you're on autopilot, it can feel so hard to take a step back and ask, "Is what I'm doing actually working for me?"

In one study, researchers asked college students to write down a list of goals they had for themselves. With such an open question, and no judgment, the researchers believed that every goal the students wrote down would be freely chosen. The students later came back to their lists and marked off whether a goal was something that they felt pressured to do or something they really, truly wanted. With a bit of distance, many of them admitted that much of what they wrote down was extrinsic. That's how autopilot works: a blank sheet of paper, no judgment, and your hopes and dreams are still not your own.

However, just like with a real-life autopilot system, you can regain your control at any moment. You're the driver. You're in charge. This is your life. Don't let autopilot run it for you. The goals that you set for yourself *matter*—they influence your daily emotions, experiences, and relationships; they shape your long-term development as a person; and they direct the course of your life.

Don't follow a set path. Look within and follow what matters to you.

Here are some proven and simple tactics that will help you get off autopilot.

Look at Your Current Destination

To take yourself off autopilot, write down on a piece of paper all of your current goals, big and small. Come back to it a bit later, and circle the goals that feel like they are truly your own. Your list might look something like this:

- Take better care of my health
- Get promoted
- Declutter the house
- Win the company award
- Spend more time with my friends/partner/kids/family
- Run a marathon

If you don't know where a goal falls, evaluate whether it will make you happy in the process of pursuing it or just at the end, when you achieve the result. "Win the company award" is about the result; "Spend more time with loved ones" is about the process.

The way you write the goal also gives you clues. "Get promoted" is an Old Happy outcome because it is about external validation; it could be reimagined as "Invest in my professional development through a course," or "Practice leadership skills to prepare to be a manager."

Agassi got himself off autopilot. He said, "Just because I didn't choose my life doesn't mean I can't take ownership of it," and started setting different goals for himself. As an eighth-grade dropout, he was passionate about giving kids access to education. At age twenty-four, he opened his first charter school in his hometown of Las Vegas. That's since expanded to a foundation that helps more than sixty-five thousand kids access an education every year.

Decide Where You Want to Go

If your autopilot has been on for a while, it's normal to feel a little bit lost when you turn it off. Asking, "What do I want?" can feel like a radical question.

What if you allowed yourself to do what you loved to do, what you enjoyed, or what you've always been curious about? Your unique hopes and dreams matter, and they are not random. They are important keys to your happiness. Pause and give yourself permission to choose a goal that really matters to you. Say to yourself, "The best goals are the ones that bring me joy along the way."

A goal that makes you happy tends to have three motivations behind it: you find it innately interesting or fun, it's personally important to you, or it reflects your values. That's why training for a 5K or saving money, although maybe not the most enjoyable things you'll ever do, can still contribute to your well-being.

Brainstorm a few goals that you would like to pursue. Here are a few examples to use as inspiration (but remember, the most important thing is to choose ones that feel right for you):

- Safety: "I want to build a savings cushion."
- Health: "I am going to train for a 5K with my friends."
- Self-acceptance: "I'm going to start saying 'no' more."
- Growth: "I want to learn how to play the violin."
- Connection: "Every Friday, I'm going to call my dad on my walk home from work."
- Community: "I would like to find a nonprofit I can donate my skills to."

If at any point you're feeling unsure, a simple reminder can help. One study found that reminding people to "Follow your heart" or "Trust your gut" helped them to turn off autopilot and set intrinsic goals.

The funny thing is that those who aim directly at joy and meaning often end up experiencing success, just as we saw with Federer. Fred Rogers once described this phenomenon: "The thing I remember best about successful people I've met all through the years is their obvious delight in what they're doing. It seems to have very little to do with worldly success. They just love what they're doing, and they love it in front of others."

TAKE AUTHENTIC ACTION

Many advertisements show "before" and "after" pictures comparing a human or a product that's been transformed. That's how Old Happy outcomes appear in your mind: your present, inadequate self on the left (the "before") and your perfect self's achievements on the right (your potential "after").

> Before: You, staring at a blank page, with writer's block.
> After: Your column on the front page of *The New York Times*.

> Before: You, working an unfulfilling office job, bored and disrespected.
> After: You, an important executive, leading your team to success.

> Before: You, lying on the couch, feeling tired.
> After: You, triumphantly finishing a marathon, a medal around your neck.

This comparison makes you desire the after picture and hate the before picture (and hate the version of yourself in the before picture, too, only further reinforcing the perfect self). Remember, Agassi's misery came from the after picture that was forced upon him: an image of the most successful tennis player of all time.

Happiness does not exist in the future. There is no future achievement that will make you lastingly happy. There is, of course, value in dreaming up a goal or a vision for yourself. But New Happy goals don't look like after pictures. They don't have a look at all. They have a feeling: warmth, hope, or purpose.

Instead of longing for an after picture, focus instead on the snapshot that you can take in the present moment—the authentic action that you can take today:

"I wonder what I would write about that topic."

"Let me find one way to help my team today."

"It would be cool to try long-distance running sometime."

Happiness is found only in the here and now, through doing things that are meaningful, joyful, and fulfilling. An authentic action is both satisfying in the short term and builds toward something meaningful in the long term. That's where Federer's joy came from—his daily snapshot, playing tennis for the love of it.

The next time you notice yourself dreaming up after pictures, you can pull yourself back into the present moment. What's the authentic action that you can take today? Write one page. Help one colleague. Lace up your running shoes.

These authentic actions help you to find happiness. They also do something else.

All of the research on extrinsic and intrinsic goals is grounded in the same insight we explored in the last chapter: your true self is good.

Within you, your true self knows exactly what it needs to be happy and feels incredibly motivated to pursue it. Once you tap into it, you'll never again have to ask, "How can I be more motivated?" You will instinctively take the unique, authentic actions that help you grow and make you feel good.

If you need more proof of your true nature, look at the names of the two types of goals.

Extrinsic is derived from the French word *extrinsèque*, which means "not of the essence or inner nature of a thing." Extrinsic goals are not aligned with who you really are. That's why they can never make you happy: they don't satisfy your true self's needs. They might be a want, sure, but wants don't make you lastingly happy because they don't touch the core of who you are.

Intrinsic, on the other hand, means "internal, inward." These goals *do* align with who you really are and *do* satisfy your real needs. Our

By taking action, you will become the person you are meant to be.

most important needs are being connected, sharing, contributing, growing, loving and being loved in return, and living in a world where it's safe to be who we really are. What is goodness, if not this?

The Polish psychologist Kazimierz Dąbrowski said that "authenticity is the drive to become attuned to our higher nature." This is what happens when you pursue New Happy goals: you attune yourself to your true self, your inner goodness.

Every time you take authentic action, you're connecting with and expanding your true self. It helps you become more and more yourself. That's the real, hidden power of pursuing New Happy goals.

You can use this new perspective as you approach all of your goals and decisions:

- When you're making a choice: Ask, "What option will help me become more of myself?"
- When you're setting a goal: Ask, "Will this help fulfill my true self's needs?"
- When you're planning your day: Ask, "What is one thing I can do today that will help me express myself?"

What makes us happiest is not "getting somewhere." What makes us happy is acting in alignment with our true selves. Happiness is something *you do*. As cliché as it sounds, it truly is about the journey—but not about the journey of getting somewhere. Rather, it's about the journey of becoming who you really are through the actions that you take.

Action is not the means to an end. It's the end in and of itself. It's how you become yourself. It's what life is made of. It's where we find our happiness.

KEY TAKEAWAYS

- The second Old Happy lie is that if you achieve certain goals, you will be happy. These goals are extrinsic and do not help you find happiness. (Sometimes they even hurt you.)

- Old Happy puts us on autopilot, steering us toward goals that hurt us. Turn off autopilot by writing down a list of your goals and then evaluating them to see which ones truly matter to you.

- Devote your goal-setting power to New Happy goals that are intrinsic and fulfill your needs. These help you experience the joy of authentic action while also working toward a meaningful objective.

- As you pursue New Happy goals, you connect with and expand your true self.

6

The Third Lie: You're on Your Own

More than two hundred fifty million years ago, in the late Paleozoic era, all of the landmasses on Earth were connected, forming a super-continent called Pangea.

Toward the end of the Triassic period, tectonic plate movements started to break Pangea apart. The pieces began to drift, millimeters at a time. During the course of millions of years, Pangea split into two, forming Laurasia and Gondwanaland. Then it split again, break-ing into the continents we know today.

We have come to see each continent as a unique, separate thing. But they were not always this way. Florida was tucked in next to Sen-egal and Guinea. Nova Scotia and Morocco were nestled together.

Old Happy culture acts like the tectonic plate movement that broke apart Pangea, separating what was once connected. Psychologically, we have never been farther apart from each other. We have forgotten the single most important factor for our happiness: the awareness that we are connected.

THE SEPARATE LIE

The third worldview question is: How am I connected to others?

Old Happy's answer: You aren't connected to anyone.

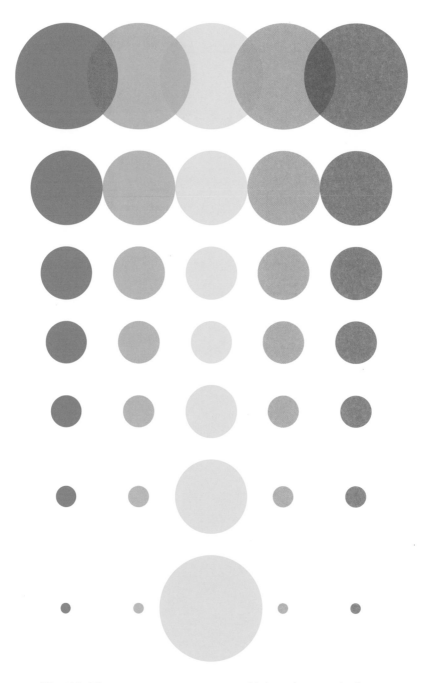

The third lie: you are on your own, which makes you believe
that you are more important than other people.

You have been told that you, as a person, are separate from others, your community, and our world. There's "you" and then "everyone outside you."

This is the belief that is most deeply embedded within our worldview. It really and truly seems like your self is completely separate from all other selves. You are in a different body, aren't you? You have your own private thoughts. You have feelings that rise and fall. You have distinct needs, desires, and dreams.

This is true. *And* it's not the full picture. "No man is an island entire of himself," wrote the poet John Donne in 1624 as he lay ill with typhus in London.

Yet this is exactly how we have been taught to view ourselves. In a seminal paper, researchers Hazel Rose Markus and Shinobu Kitayama argued that the way you see yourself is highly shaped by your culture. Those of us who grow up in individualistic cultures see the self in a completely different way than those who grow up in collectivist cultures.

We are taught to value ourselves for our ability to uphold individualistic ideals like achieving, being unique, and figuring things out on our own. When we describe ourselves, we use words that showcase how special and different we are: "I'm smart," or "I'm successful," or "I'm good at sports." The Buddhist philosopher Alan Watts called this our tendency to think of ourselves as "skin-encapsulated egos."

The poet T. S. Eliot, in an introduction to Dante's *Inferno*, wrote: "Hell is a place where nothing connects with nothing." The separate lie has turned our world into a hell of our own.

We care about the things we are connected to. When you're separate from others, you don't have to care about anyone or anything beyond yourself. Even your closest bonds can be loosened, as when a sick or struggling friend or relative becomes a burden that interferes with your personal goals. A person sleeping on the street is something to step around and ignore. A faraway country facing the consequences of global warming gets a second of our attention before we head to work in our gas-guzzling car.

This adds up to a culture in which everyone is compelled to look out solely for themselves. Do what you want to do, when you want to do it, with no regard for the impact upon others. Living separately pits you against others, rather than aligning you with them. It has created a world in which people are used and tossed aside or seen as a means to an end. It transforms life into an endless competition because nothing is shared and everything has to be won for yourself. This self-focused pursuit of success is not questioned by our culture. It's celebrated. It drives us to pursue extrinsic goals and to seek to become the perfect self.

For further evidence, look at how we treat people when they're struggling. They're told to fix themselves—on their own. They need to change themselves, develop new habits, and otherwise focus on themselves until they are "better." What is better? Being strong, independent, and no longer needing any help. Separate. It's rare that the ecosystem surrounding them is explored: what social, cultural, or environmental conditions might be making this person unhappy? When someone you love is struggling, do you ask yourself, "How am I contributing to their pain?" Most of us don't. It's their pain, in their own little skin-encapsulated ego, and, therefore, it's their problem.

Another example: parents. One study estimated that 66 percent of working American parents meet the criteria for parental burnout. They feel intensely exhausted and question their ability to be good parents. To cope, they disconnect from their kids, losing the joy and meaning of parenting, which amplifies their stress and exhaustion even further.

In a landmark study, scientists discovered that individualistic countries are by far the most likely to have burnt-out parents. In the United States, there's a profound lack of infrastructure supporting parents and caregivers. Writing for *The Atlantic*, Kendra Hurley pointed out that this stems from the belief that "good" parents are those who do it all on their own and that "government support for parents is at odds with

When we are separate, we have to carry
all of our burdens by ourselves.

parents being responsible for their kids." The scientist leading this study, Isabelle Roskam, pointed to Old Happy culture as the cause: "Our individualistic countries cultivate a cult of performance and perfectionism. Parenthood in these countries is a very solitary activity."

When you are separate, you are solely responsible for absolutely everything that happens within you, to you, and for you. That includes your happiness. You are on your own.

Yet this flies in the face of years of research. We are deeply affected by the world around us.

Scientists all agree that the single most important factor for your long-term happiness is your connections. The longest-running study at Harvard has followed the lives of 724 men for more than eighty years. The key finding? The happiest men were those who were the most connected to others.

When we are disconnected, terrible things happen to our health. Loneliness is more deadly than smoking and inactivity; it increases your risk of dementia by 50 percent, and it's associated with greater risks of premature death and mental health challenges.

Look at how we punish people in prisons, using solitary confinement and depriving people of human contact, which leads to severe psychological harm. One study found that those in solitary confinement reported twice as many symptoms of trauma as other incarcerated people and were seven times more likely to harm themselves. Many human rights advocates argue that it's a form of torture.

The science is clear: the more connected you are, the healthier and happier you tend to be. The more disconnected you are, the more unwell and unhappy you tend to be.

Why? We are in no way, shape, or form separate from one another. Reconnecting is our task; happiness is our reward.

A SELF NEEDS OTHER SELVES

The constant discontentment of Old Happy comes from the fact that it denies another truth of our nature: not only are we good people who need to express ourselves through authentic action, but we are also deeply connected with others.

Those who come face-to-face with their mortality are desperate to tell us this. Three hundred ninety-six years after John Donne penned his poem, a young man named Elliot Dallen was dying of cancer in the same city. In a moving piece for *The Guardian*, he echoed Donne's words saying that before his diagnosis he believed himself to be completely independent; however, along the way, as he experienced the ups and downs of living with a terminal illness, Elliot understood Donne's words 'No Man is an Island' for the first time. He was humbled to discover how much he did indeed depend on other people, not just physically, but emotionally too. He realised that ultimately it is the people you love who get you through the hard times.

This is the ultimate irony of the separate lie. We believe ourselves to be completely independent, but the self is created and defined by its interactions and relationships with other people.

Babies do not believe that they are separate beings from their caregivers until they're a few months old. As they get older, they begin to develop their "selves" through their relationships with the people around them. We even develop our views of ourselves based on how others see us, a phenomenon that sociologists call the "looking-glass" self.

Our brains are designed to be in relationship with one another. Just like we need food and sleep to survive, so, too, do we need social interaction. As we grow up, our brains develop through interacting with one another and the world around us. Neuroscientists point out that we are intrinsically motivated to pursue these connections and that we feel anxious and upset when we don't have them in our lives.

Once our selves are more developed, they continue being affected by others and the world around us. For example, as I write this today, I'm tired and heartsick because I stayed up far too late crying over yesterday's Russian invasion of Ukraine. I'm lonely because I have been in pandemic isolation for more than two years, due to govern-

ment policies that don't protect disabled people. I'm overjoyed looking at photos of a dear friend's wedding. Yet I'm supposed to believe I
am separate from my friends, my community, and the world?

As we experience emotions, they become contagious, too. One paper estimated that between 80 and 95 percent of the time you have an
emotional experience, you share it with someone else. In one famous
study, researchers looked at a network of nearly five thousand people
over twenty years and mapped out all of their social connections to
one another, identifying more than fifty thousand relationships. They
discovered that, when one person in the study was happy, it kicked off
a chain reaction—that person's connections became happier and then
their connections became happier, too. Your happiness is affected by
people you have never met before.

As we have become connected in new ways, our influence on one
another has expanded even further. In one experiment, researchers
manipulated the posts shared in Facebook's feed. When there was
more negative content in people's feeds, they were more likely to post
negative updates. When there was more positive content in people's
feeds, they were more likely to post positive updates.

There is no "me" without "we."

FIND THE OVERLAP

Changing the way we view ourselves, from separate to connected, is
something we can start to do right here and now.

I call it creating an overlap. You naturally overlap in times like
these:

- Going out for a hike and being awed by nature
- Watching someone you love get married
- Celebrating a community's achievement
- Getting a hug from your child
- Observing a piece of art that touches you to your core
- Laughing with a friend

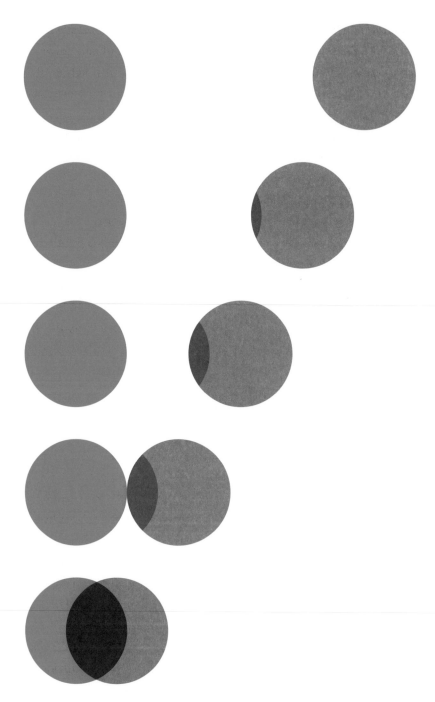

Reconnect by looking for the ways in which you overlap with others.

- Mourning a tragedy with loved ones
- Watching your team or country win a sporting event

We're used to creating an overlap with the people we love. When you build a close relationship with someone, you naturally start to adopt parts of them as your own. That's one reason why falling in romantic love is such a rush: all of a sudden, the false separation is gone! It feels like you're merged with the person you love. The overlap even transforms your brain; one study found that when an individual heard a close friend's name, they experienced a similar brain response pattern as when they heard their own name.

You already know how to do this. Now, you can start doing it intentionally by practicing seeing other people as *people*; see their humanity rather than their utility.

Imagine yourself as a circle, separate and alone. Another person is a different, separate circle. How can we get them to overlap and connect?

Method #1:
Look for Another Person's Goodness

Just like you, everyone has a true self within them. Take a moment to seek out another person's goodness.

- With a friend: reflect on a lesson that they taught you or a nice compliment that they once gave you.
- With a coworker: think about the last time they helped you with a project or when they did a great job helping a customer.
- With a child: recall their expressions of love, like a picture they drew for you or the way they run to hug you.

Method #2:
Focus on What You Share

Researchers have discovered that using "we" language ("How can we do this?" or "What will make us happy?") can help you shift from separate to connected. Look at this person and ask yourself, "What do we have in common?"

- With a grumpy coworker: reflect on a time you felt grumpy, too.
- With your partner: think about the difficult experiences you've gotten through together and the joyful times you have shared.
- With a stranger: think about how this is a person, just like you, who is striving to live a good life, who experiences pain, who is facing many challenges, and who just wants to be happy, too.

Method #3:
Do Something Together

Another way to overlap is to move synchronously with another person or engage in group activities.

- With your kids: play catch or a game.
- With your friends: dance, sing, or hike together.
- With your team at work: schedule time to brainstorm solutions to a tough problem.

These activities change our behavior, making us more likely to trust the other person and help them. It even works with children: one study found that when four-year-old children make music together, they're more likely to cooperate and help each other afterward.

One overlap at a time, we can start to reconnect with others and reap the benefits. I love the way the painter Vincent van Gogh described this connection in a letter that he wrote to his beloved brother Theo in 1880: "Do you know what frees one from captivity? It is every deep, serious affection. Being friends, being brothers, love, this is what opens the prison by some supreme power, by some magic force. Without this, one remains in prison. Where sympathy is renewed, life is restored."

EXPAND YOUR OVERLAP USING QUESTIONS

This key principle of overlapping is central to religious, spiritual, and moral teachings. Yet even the leaders of these groups can struggle with breaking down their boundaries. We're all human.

I once heard a story about this from the professor David Cooperrider. In the late 1990s, he was asked to bring together the world's religious leaders to engage in an open conversation. Some of these religions had not communicated in more than four hundred years.

The night before the event, there was tension in the air. Cooperrider overheard a bishop expressing his concerns and apprehension about the meeting, saying that he didn't know if it was a good idea.

The next day, the twenty leaders all gathered in a room. Cooperrider divided them into pairs. They were told to ask one another, "Can you share a story of a moment, or of the period of time, when clarity about life's purpose emerged for you? What do you sense you are supposed to do before your life is over?" After discussing, they came back together as a group, with each person introducing their partner to the room and sharing a little bit of their story.

That bishop, who had expressed so much apprehension about the summit, was called up to introduce his partner. He looked nervous, like he didn't know what to do. Finally, he put his hand around his partner's shoulder and spluttered out, "I just want to say—I just want to say—I love this man!"

By asking another person questions and listening to them, you're not just expanding your overlap. You're also connecting to your own true self, enabling you to see the other person with so much more love. Yes, this person might be different from you in some ways, but they are also, in so many other ways, very much the same.

There's an exercise that's repeatedly been studied called the "Fast Friends procedure," which pairs two complete strangers to answer thirty-six questions that slowly escalate in intimacy.

It starts out with questions like, "Before making a telephone call, do you ever rehearse what you are going to say? Why?" Then it moves on to more personal ones like, "Is there something that you've dreamed of doing for a long time? Why haven't you done it?" And it ends with intimate questions like, "Tell your partner what you like about them. Be very honest this time, saying things that you might not say to someone you've just met."

Using these questions can create feelings of closeness and friendship in less than an hour. Some participants said that, after the conversation, their new friends knew more about them than their closest family and friends. One pair from the original experiment even fell in love and got married.

This is a stunning finding: our questions define our ability to overlap with one another and, therefore, shape our happiness. We can't leave this in the lab; we have to bring it to our lives. The key is to try to ask questions that bring out another person's true self. They can be as simple as these:

- How are you really feeling?
- What brought you joy today?
- Is there something you're looking forward to in the coming days?
- Can you tell me a story about . . . ?
- What are you feeling proud of yourself for?
- What's hard right now?
- What do you need?

It can feel vulnerable to open up to connection, especially if you have been hurt before. We've all experienced how painful it is to feel used, discarded, or rejected for our humanity. The fact that we've all felt this pain can become a powerful motivation to try to ensure no one else feels this way. With your actions, you can help prevent these negative experiences for other people or heal them after they have happened.

YOU ARE CONNECTED

The separate lie tells you that you can't be yourself and be connected to others at the same time, that you must free yourself of all relation-

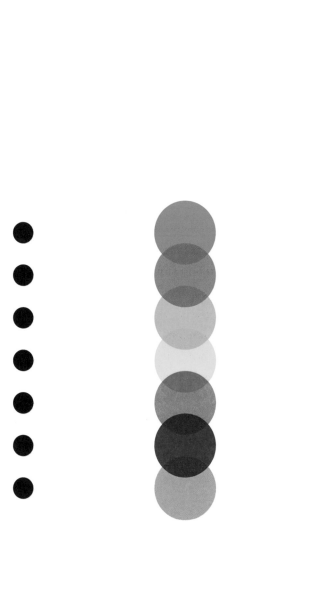

Your relationships help you to be who you are
and to grow as a person.

ships and responsibilities. In reality, our connections are what help us to be who we truly are and become all we can be. As John Donne wrote farther on in his poem, "Every man is a piece of the Continent, a part of the main." We are both—our own, individual selves and inextricably connected to others.

The things that we as individuals want for ourselves—being the best we can be, growing as people, making a difference, and feeling happiness—are enabled by our connections to others.

When are you at your best as a person? When you are deeply, truly concerned about another.

How are you able to grow as a person? By learning from those who came before you, collaborating, and getting feedback.

How are you able to make a difference in the world? Through what you give to others, for without other people, you could never fall in love, have children, impart wisdom, contribute to a greater purpose, make a difference, or even make someone laugh.

There's a famous quote from Jean-Paul Sartre's play *No Exit*: "Hell is other people." It's been used over the years to justify a doctrine of separation. What many people don't know is that in a later interview, Sartre elaborated on this statement. He said that this is only one side of the coin. The other side, which is never recognized, is that "heaven is each other." The defining nature of hell, he explains, is separateness, which results in selfishness, an obsession with power, and the accumulation of wealth. The defining nature of heaven, on the other hand, is that of care, mutuality, and collectivity.

I have to agree with Sartre – we find our happiness together.

A NEW WORLDVIEW NEEDS
A NEW APPROACH

Throughout the past three chapters, we have unwound the three Old Happy lies and explored how these unwritten instructions taught us to hate and punish ourselves for our humanity, pursue goals that make us unhappy, and lose sight of our connectedness.

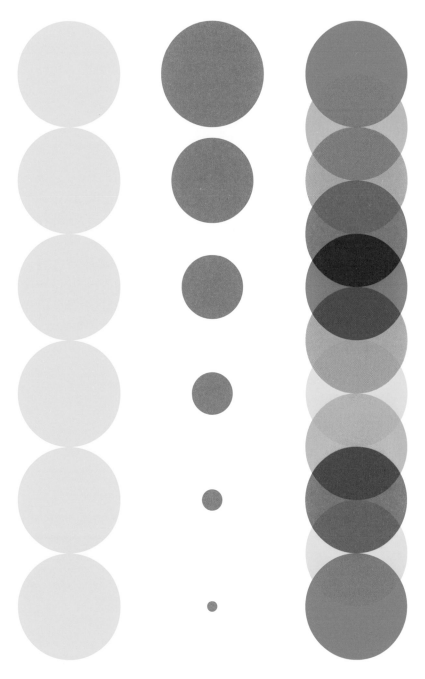

The New Happy worldview: you are enough, you grow through
authentic action, and you are connected to others.

In their place, we have begun to build a New Happy worldview, with new answers to these three key questions:

Who are you? Worthy, just as you are.

What should you do? Take authentic action.

How are you related to others? You are connected.

When you look at the world in this very different way, it inspires you to want to pursue a very different type of life. Suddenly, the idea of seeking to be perfect, of striving for more and more, and of doing it all by yourself seems irrational and foolish. It doesn't work, and it's hurting you and everyone else. There must be a better way to live.

There is.

There is a simple secret to happiness, one that winds all three of these beliefs together, that will bring you the lasting joy you have been looking for. That's where we will turn our attention next.

KEY TAKEAWAYS

- The third Old Happy lie is that you are separate from others.

- Being connected is essential to happiness.

- Create an overlap with the people in your life by seeing their strengths, focusing on what you share, doing activities together, and asking questions.

- Our individual potential can only be unlocked through our relationships with one another.

- The New Happy worldview helps you understand that you're enough as you are, you grow through authentic action, and you are connected to others.

PART THREE

Understand Happiness

7

The Fundamental Truth
About Happiness

In Milwaukee, Wisconsin, there's a small consulting firm that unknowingly changed the way we think about happiness.

Back in 1943, the humanistic psychologist Abraham Maslow published his groundbreaking work "A Theory of Human Motivation." In this paper, he argued that humans have five core needs: physiological, safety, love, esteem, and self-actualization.

Many of us know this theory as the famous Hierarchy of Needs. It puts these human needs into a pyramid, with physiological at the bottom and self-actualization at the top. The pyramid has become a major part of our culture; it shows up in every psychology textbook, has been replicated on the internet in countless manifestations, and is collectively acknowledged as solid fact.

But here's the truth: Maslow never put his needs into this pyramid shape.

In a fascinating paper, researchers Todd Bridgman, Stephen Cummings, and John Ballard investigated how Maslow's academic paper became a pyramid. It was built like a game of telephone. One person read Maslow's paper and simplified it, getting it a little bit wrong. Then another person used that new source, and it changed a little bit more. Finally, it ended with a group of consultants at Humber,

Mundie & McClary, the consulting firm in Milwaukee, who turned it into the visual pyramid we all know.

This evolution of knowledge happens all the time. I don't blame the consultants; I know how hard it is to accurately translate concepts to visuals! The problem is that the pyramid has become a meme, a piece of cultural information that changes the way we see the world and guides our behavior.

Another pyramid you might remember? The infamous US food pyramid. At the bottom of the former nutritional guide were rice, pasta, bread, and cereal, of which you were supposed to eat six to eleven servings per day. At the next level were fruits (two to four servings) and vegetables (three to five servings), followed by meat, beans, nuts, eggs, and dairy (two or three servings each), topped with fats, sweets, and oils ("use sparingly"). The pyramid guided our eating behavior, even though it wasn't accurate: it was influenced by lobbyists who wanted to sell their products. Some experts have argued that the pyramid contributed to rising obesity levels by promoting a diet high in refined carbohydrates.

Just as the food pyramid shaped the choices we made about health, Maslow's pyramid has shaped the choices we make about happiness.

HOW THE PYRAMID REINFORCES OLD HAPPY

When Old Happy is our definition of happiness, we look at Maslow's pyramid and see an image that reinforces the three lies.

You Have to Climb to the Top

The pyramid immediately creates a hierarchy. You start at the bottom and have to work your way to the top by progressing through the different levels. Those who can reach the top are deemed worthy of pursuing self-actualization; those who can't fulfill their lower-level needs aren't "allowed" to.

A public health professor at the University of Michigan named Vic Strecher once shared a story on this topic. He was working in Uganda

Your needs are not a pyramid to climb. All of your needs matter
and you are constantly in the process of fulfilling them.

and made friends with a man named James Arinaitwe, who became an orphan at the age of five when both his parents died of AIDS. Strecher describes having a conversation with Arinaitwe one day, asking him what he thought about our Western conceptualization of purpose that is derived from Maslow's pyramid: that it's something that you can pursue when you have fulfilled all of your other needs. Arinaitwe, laughing, responded that this couldn't be further from the truth. People who have nothing, he said, need hope more than anything, and that hope comes from caring about something beyond themselves. He shared how his own purpose has helped him to fulfill his own potential and show up for the people in his life. Purpose, Arinaitwe says, is absolutely essential.

In his paper, though, Maslow writes that most people are partially satisfied and partially unsatisfied in all of their needs, all at the same time:

> . . . if I may assign arbitrary figures for the sake of illustration, it is as if the average citizen is satisfied perhaps 85 per cent in his physiological needs, 70 per cent in his safety needs, 50 per cent in his love needs, 40 per cent in his self-esteem needs, and 10 per cent in his self-actualization needs.

There's no "getting to the top." We are all pursuing all of our needs, all at the same time. Spending time with friends isn't only a love need—it also supports your physical health and self-esteem. Cooking dinner isn't only a health need—it also makes the home a safe space and connects you to your family. Finding a new job isn't only a security need—it also gives you health insurance, establishes new relationships, and helps you reach your potential.

The Top Glorifies Extrinsic Goals

The first four needs are clear and unambiguous. We all know how it feels to need food and water, safety, love, and self-esteem.

The fifth need, self-actualization, is another fuzzy concept like happiness, one that's vulnerable to our worldview-tinted interpretations. *Actualize* was a word invented by the poet Samuel Taylor Coleridge in 1810, meaning "to make actual" or "to make real." When you pair it with *self*, it means "to fulfill your potential."

Through an Old Happy lens, what's self-actualization? Achieving extrinsic goals like fame, power, and money. Yet in his paper, Maslow described self-actualization as taking authentic action that is motivated by your true self—exactly what you already learned how to do in chapter 5.

Self-actualization is not about what you get. It's about who you are.

The Pyramid Separates You

The pyramid is all about you and your individual needs. There's no mention here of your connections to others or to your greater environment.

It turns out, though, that the pyramid is missing a need.

In a seminal paper, the psychologist Mark Koltko-Rivera pointed out that in his later writings, Maslow admitted he had made a grave error: he had forgotten to include the sixth need, for self-transcendence.

Where self-actualization is about becoming the fullest expression of yourself, self-transcendence is about going beyond yourself, connecting with others, and identifying with something bigger than you. We find it through being of service to others, through pursuing a purpose that helps people, or through spiritual experiences.

The most famous model of human needs doesn't even mention the need to go beyond our self-interest. It's no wonder that helping other people is seen as an optional "nice-to-have." The highest pinnacle of human achievement, the greatest thing to aspire to, seems to be self-focused personal success. Because of this, we think of moral leaders, do-gooders, and helpers as "the exception" to the rest of the human race. In reality, they're more tuned in to their real needs than we are.

What does this teach us? Your happiness comes first. You don't have to help anyone until all your needs are satisfied. This leads to a common idea in Old Happy culture, something that I call the "get rich first" approach:

"I'll help people when I'm rich and successful."

"I'll help people in the second half of my life."

"It's moral for me to pursue excessive wealth because I plan to donate some of it."

But as Maslow said, all of your needs will never be satisfied.

This leaves us spending our lives trying to climb to the top of our respective personal pyramids, while missing the secret to happiness that would be staring us all in the face if it weren't for an inaccurate illustration with a poorly chosen shape: If you want to be happy, you can't ignore the sixth need. You have to help people.

WE ARE WIRED TO HELP

Going beyond ourselves is a need, just like sleep, food, love, and esteem are needs. That's why it feels good when we help people, just like it feels good when we get a good night's sleep, or drink a big glass of water on a hot day, or do well on a project.

Our desire to help appears at a young age. In one study, researchers followed a sample of babies from three months old to eighteen months old. A researcher would fake an injury in front of a baby, pretending to hurt their knee and then moan about how badly it hurt. Babies as young as three months old showed concern for the hurt researcher. By the time they were eighteen months old, the babies were actively striving to help people who were suffering, motivated not by incentives or punishment, but by genuine concern for the other's well-being. The babies offered physical comfort, found someone else who could help, or gave a favorite object to the person in distress. (Much like adults do.)

Our brains reward us when we help other people. An effect known as "the helper's high," it's an activation of your mesolimbic system, which is the part of your brain that responds to food or sex. Neurotransmitters like oxytocin and vasopressin are released that make you feel good and reduce your stress hormones. Donating to charity stimulates the same neurological response that receiving money does.

Research shows that helping is also intricately connected to fulfilling your other needs. It's associated with longevity, stress reduction, and psychological well-being. Contributing to community welfare and safety leads to personal growth, purpose, and life satisfaction up to thirteen years later. The more help shared within a relationship, the more satisfied you tend to be with it. And helping others is one of the most effective ways to increase your self-worth and confidence.

We help each other even in the worst of times. One survey of World War II concentration camp survivors found that 82 percent of those interred had helped another person during their imprisonment. In his groundbreaking book *Man's Search for Meaning*, Viktor Frankl described how he survived the horrors of Auschwitz by keeping sight of a greater purpose beyond himself.

When two planes crashed into the World Trade Center's Twin Towers on September 11, 2001, tens of thousands of people ran not from the terror, but toward it. Many of the emergency systems went down, so amateur radio operators set up a network to coordinate relief. Boat owners spontaneously took their tugboats, yachts, and ferries to rescue those stranded in Lower Manhattan, transporting half a million people to safety. Hundreds of people formed bucket brigades, clearing more than one hundred thousand tons of debris within a few weeks. People donated blood, sat with grieving families, prepared food, and passed out supplies. Thousands of children wrote thank-you notes to firefighters and other first responders. So many people actually tried to help that, when things had stabilized somewhat, the agencies had a hard time getting them to go home.

Some of these volunteers were interviewed about their experiences. All described how, when they witnessed the attack, they felt the absolute need to help. One young person, who sat with grieving families, said, they wanted and needed to do it. Another person described how helping eliminated their sense of separation. They said that there was a sense of connection and togetherness that arose as a result of living through this event and being of service. An analyst who transported supplies said that volunteering was one of the most meaningful days of his life because he felt so connected to others and knew that his actions mattered.

When you're going through something hard, helping someone else really helps you, too. One study took people with depression and anxiety and split them into three groups for a five-week program. The first group was taught how to challenge their automatic thoughts. The second group was told to plan social activities every week. The third group was instructed to do three acts of kindness a day, twice a week. The third group saw the greatest improvement in well-being, both five weeks and ten weeks later.

The author Barbara Kingsolver summed up the connection between helping and happiness: "The difference between happy people and unhappy ones is that happy people have found a use for themselves, like a good tool."

This is the secret to happiness. Helping makes us happy. We are here to help each other.

HELPING IS GOOD FOR YOU
AND FOR OTHERS

In one episode of the television show *Friends*, one of the characters, Joey, argues that there is no such thing as a selfless good deed. Every time that you help someone else, you get something in return. Because it makes you feel good, it's ultimately selfish to help others.

His friend, Phoebe, is appalled by this cynical opinion. She tries to prove him wrong by doing all sorts of different good deeds. Every time, though, she discovers it helps her, too.

We are always helping each other. That's how we fulfill our own
and each other's needs. It's the only way that we can be happy.

She describes one attempt: "You know that old guy that lives next to me? Well, I snuck over there and raked up all of the leaves on his front stoop. But he caught me and force-fed me cider and cookies. Then I felt wonderful. That old jackass!"

The words *selfish* and *selfless* are frequently thrown around when we talk about helping. But these words are only relevant if we see ourselves as separate from others.

In a world where we are separate, giving is a zero-sum game. If I give something to you, it is taken away from me and now belongs to you. That's why when I say that the secret to happiness is "helping," people often express a sense of defensiveness: they feel that they have to protect themselves and their well-being. We've been conditioned to believe that if you give, you'll soon be left with nothing for yourself. In some cases, such as with money or possessions, this might be true. Most of the time, though, we are giving of ourselves.

In a world where we are connected, what you give to me is not taken away from you. When you make me smile, you get to feel good. When you help your friend with a problem, you get a stronger friendship. When you speak up for a cause, you get a sense of purpose.

Service is neither selfless nor selfish when we are connected to each other. Doing good helps you and helps others at the same time. Those volunteers who ran toward ground zero on 9/11? They did it because the tragedy showed them how connected they were. In their interviews, they describe feeling compelled to help because they knew it would benefit themselves *and* others.

We can learn a lesson from sunflowers. When a sunflower grows in a patch by itself, it sends its roots as deep as it can, seeking out the most nutrient-rich patches of soil. It pursues what is best for its own well-being. But if another sunflower is nearby, neither will sink its roots as deeply. The plants recognize that they are now a part of an ecosystem with other sunflowers and that they need to share the soil's resources. Both sunflowers can thrive at the same time.

We, too, as human beings, are sharing one patch. We, too, can share the soil, at no cost to our own well-being, and bloom together.

Service is not suffering. It's joy. You can help others and feel good at the same time. If helping is hurting your well-being, then I hope you will make adjustments. It is also not accepting mistreatment from others in any way. You will never serve the world by being harmed.

Service is not saving other people. It's making a contribution. You are not responsible for how another person feels. However, because we are all connected, we are all responsible for contributing to others' well-being where we can, when we can, and in the ways that we can.

Service is not subordination or domination. It's interdependence. Everyone needs help. The person who helps is not "better" or "worse" than the person who receives help. There's no "most valuable" way to help. We are bound together, and we all have our unique way to contribute.

Service does not define your self-worth. It's a way to express yourself. You are choosing to share your gifts with the world, but you are *always* worthy, exactly as you are. There will be times when you might need to change how you help or accept more help than you have previously. That's completely normal and a part of living in a connected world with one another.

YOU CAN HELP RIGHT NOW

I saw just how ingrained these beliefs are in our culture when I started The New Happy, about six months after Alex fell ill. We spent a whole weekend brainstorming ideas for a name. None of them felt right. Finally, late one Sunday night, Alex asked me what I had titled my master's thesis. When I told him that it was titled "A New Perspective on Happiness", he looked at me and said, "That's it! It's New Happy."

As Alex grew sicker and sicker, the New Happy movement grew more and more. As the years passed, people who cared about me were always asking, "Are you taking on too much with running The New Happy alongside your job?" "Are you sure you don't want to focus

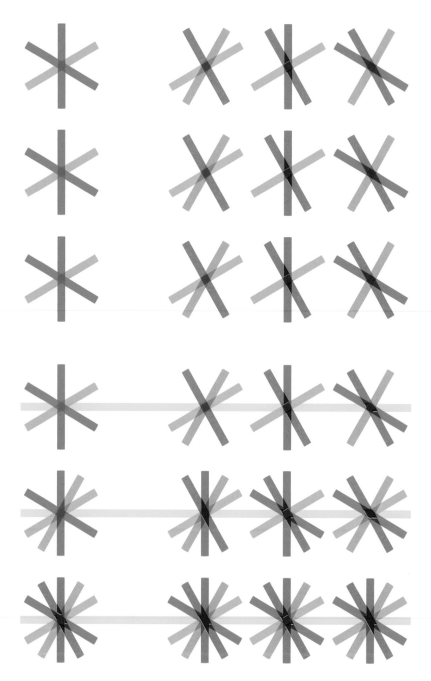

Helping people is what satisfies yours and others' needs.

Don't wait to help — help now.

more on yourself and your well-being instead?" They were so well-intentioned and just trying to help.

But I was seeing it from a totally different perspective because of what I had learned about happiness. It was my lifeline, refueling me, giving me meaning, and connecting me to others. The more I gave, the more I personally received in return. I am certain that I would not have survived those difficult years without it. I am so grateful that I didn't wait until life was better. If I had, I would still be waiting, and I would have missed out on so much joy.

As Maslow himself said, you are never going to satisfy all of your other needs fully and absolutely. If you're waiting for that, you'll be waiting for the rest of your life. So don't wait to help. Help *now*.

Together with our community, The New Happy put together a Help Now toolkit, full of small ways we can help one another. Here is an excerpt; read through the list, choose one, or come up with your own. Then put this book down and go do it.

Loved ones:
- Call a friend you haven't spoken to in a while.
- Send a note to someone telling them how you appreciate them.
- Help your family or roommate with a chore.

Work:
- Write a kind email praising someone's work.
- Try to turn around someone's day through kindness.
- Drop off extra food for a colleague going through a hard time.

Community:
- Call a store or business that you have benefitted from to thank them.
- Knock on a neighbor's door to check in.

- Reach out to someone you admire, and let them know how they've influenced you.

World:
- Smile at a stranger.
- Sign a petition on change.org.
- Speak up about a cause that matters to you.

(You can find the full toolkit and submit your suggestions on our website, thenewhappy.com/helpnow.)

You never have to wait to be happy because there is always someone out there you can help.

KEY TAKEAWAYS

- Maslow never made his famous pyramid.

- The pyramid became a meme that reinforces Old Happy and prevents us from seeing the secret to happiness: helping each other.

- We have a deep need to help one another. Not only does helping lead to happiness, it can even help us to satisfy our other needs.

- Helping is the ultimate win-win: it makes two people happier.

- When you're feeling unhappy or down, take a few minutes to help another person.

8

The Helping Paradox

Michael Phelps is the most decorated Olympian of all time, with twenty-eight medals to his name. To achieve that, he had to do a lot of hard things.

He started his day by diving into a freezing cold pool. He spent six or seven hours a day training, swimming more than eighty thousand yards every week in the pool. He could never pause or slow down: the day after his first Olympics concluded, he hopped straight back in the pool to start training for the next Games—1,412 days away. Even his recovery time was painful, as he plunged his body into tubs of ice and did something called Graston, a technique using "a set of metal tools that essentially kicks the living crap out of you."

Yet he says that one of the hardest things he ever did was learn how to ask for help.

He isn't alone. I have never spoken to a single person who finds it easy to ask for help. This struggle is, once again, rooted in the Old Happy worldview:

- The lack lie tells you that you need to be perfect to be worthy. But the perfect self never struggles. This means that if you're having a hard time, something is wrong with you.
- The outcome lie tells you that external achievements will

make you happy. If you can just "get there," all of your pain and suffering will go away.

- The separate lie tells you that you can't depend on people, and you are solely responsible for solving your problems. Other people can't (or don't want to) help you.

Old Happy makes hard times so much harder. It doesn't need to be this way.

YOU ARE ENOUGH WHEN YOU ARE STRUGGLING

After Phelps retired from swimming, he found a new purpose: mental health awareness and access. In a recent interview, he looked back on his time as an athlete and described how much the perfect self hurt him: "I used to hate who I saw in the mirror. The only thing I saw was a swimmer. I never saw myself as a human being."

It's not only athletes who struggle with this. One study looked at caregivers of family members with dementia—a group that has a notoriously difficult time asking for help. Every time they felt sad about their situation, or frustrated with their ill loved one, or made a mistake, they saw themselves as a "bad" caregiver. Their ongoing comparisons to the perfect self led to a perpetual sense of guilt and a reluctance to lean on others.

If your worldview taught you that receiving help makes you an unacceptable person, what are you supposed to do when you're struggling? Your self-worth is based on *not* needing help. How many of us pretend we're okay, engage in unhealthy behaviors, or distance ourselves from support rather than ask for what we need?

Instead of hating ourselves for our very real, normal, human struggles, we need to treat ourselves with kindness. One of the most effective ways to do this is by learning to look at ourselves with loving eyes.

Imagine, as vividly as you can, someone who is struggling—someone who is lonely, who doesn't have enough money to pay their

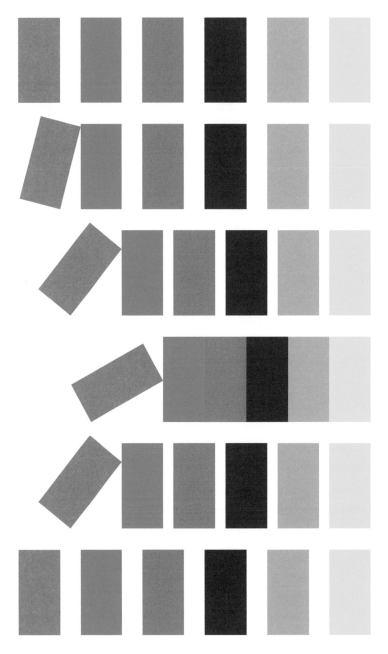

Everyone goes through difficult times. The people in your life
can support you and help you get back on your feet.

rent, who is feeling left out, who feels inadequate, who is heartbroken, who is ill. Feel compassion building within you as you see this person who deserves help and love. You'll probably feel your eyes softening.

Now, turn that gaze upon yourself. Here, too, is a person who deserves help and love. Look at yourself with those loving eyes. There's nothing you need to prove, nothing you need to change, and nothing you need to do differently. You are worthy in your most painful moments.

As you learned in chapter 4, you can always access your true self, an ever-present source of love and compassion. When I am having a hard time, I'll often take a deep breath and say, "What would my true self say to me right now?" or "What is something that I need to hear right now?" These simple sentences have the extraordinary power to connect you with your true self. Remember: you can't hurt yourself into a state of greater happiness; you can only love yourself into a state of greater happiness.

Part of loving yourself involves knowing that you are worthy of help. Hear this: you can't really be living a New Happy life if you are not receiving help from other people.

If you're only giving, you're simply dressing up Old Happy in a different outfit. You're on the outside looking in, not participating in the ebb and flow of interconnectedness. If you accept that happiness comes from helping other people, you also must accept that, as a person, you need to receive help.

The language we use in giving and receiving shows how much Old Happy has informed our beliefs about asking for help, with phrases like, "I don't want to be a burden," or "I'm not a fun person to be around right now," or "I'm worried that I'm draining you."

Human beings do not possess a finite amount of love, compassion, and support. If you ask someone for love, you are not draining them of their limited supply. People are not oil wells. Care is not a nonrenewable resource. You can ask people for help. You are not sucking them dry.

To the contrary, asking for help gives someone else a chance to be of service and, therefore, to experience happiness.

This is what I call the helping paradox: when you ask for help, you are helping. Wherever there is a need, there are two chances for happiness: one for the person with the need and one for the person fulfilling it.

We are here to help each other. That "we" includes you. The ocean has waves; birds have wings; humans have needs. It's no shame to need help; it is who we are.

Many of us need to relearn how to ask for help. I recommend creating what I call a "Signal List." These are the signals that your body, mind, and heart give you to let you know that you need help from other people. Write down your Signal List in a journal or on your phone, where you can refer to it when you need it.

To come up with your signals, think back to a time that you were struggling. What were you experiencing?

Body

Here are some of the most common bodily distress signals, as cited by doctors and therapists:

- Experiencing a change in eating habits
- Having difficulty sleeping
- Sleeping too much
- Feeling generally fatigued and exhausted
- Feeling overly anxious
- Experiencing physical pain
- Having trouble remembering things

Emotions

One of the most important lessons I have ever learned came from Marshall Rosenberg, a psychologist who created a technique called nonviolent communication.

Rosenberg taught that emotions are information about whether our needs are being met. Your emotions are not something to demonize or be afraid of, nor are they the objective truth about your life. They are data that can indicate how things are going.

What feelings come up for you when you are having a hard time?

- Anger
- Anxiety
- Fear
- Frustration
- Helplessness

- Hurt
- Jealousy
- Loneliness
- Sadness
- Shame

When you feel these emotions, it is something to pay attention to, a signal that indicates, "I might need something."

Behaviors

If you have a hard time noticing these inner experiences, you also can look at your outer behaviors. Your thoughts and emotions influence what you do, providing you with another way to discern your needs. For example, I love singing in the car or in my house. But when I am struggling, I stop doing it. Now I know that this is a signal I need to attend to.

Here are a few other behaviors that might be signals:

- Disconnecting from people who care about you
- Skipping events or routines that you enjoy
- Beating yourself up more frequently
- Talking about other people in negative ways
- Overconsuming media

You could even turn your Signal List into a checklist. In *The Checklist Manifesto*, the surgeon Atul Gawande describes how his team asked clinicians in eight hospitals around the world to use a nineteen-step checklist to improve patient outcomes. Many of them grumbled, saying it was unnecessary. But it ended up having a huge impact: postsurgical deaths decreased by 47 percent. Having a reminder in front of you can make all of the difference. Every week, go through your Signal List and ask yourself, "Have I noticed any of these signals lately?" Take it to the next level by going through your checklist with your roommates or your family. This will make it easier to be better helpers for each other.

You now know *when* to ask for help. Next comes the harder part: actually doing the asking. The words can get stuck in our throats: "I need help."

Sometimes, you might not know what exactly you need help with. If you're already struggling, figuring out what you need can be so hard. Remember, you don't have to be the perfect self who asks for help in the perfect way. Reach out to someone and say something like, "I need help, but I don't know what I need help with. Could you ask me a few questions and help me figure it out?" Let someone join you in your pain. You don't have to go it alone.

If you do know what you need, the best strategy is to be clear and direct:

- With your partner: "It would help me if you could cook all of the family meals this week."
- With your boss: "I am struggling with this project and need your help brainstorming a path forward."
- With a mentor: "Do you have ten minutes to review my résumé?"

People *want* to help us. Vanessa Bohns, a psychologist at Cornell University, got study participants to make more than fourteen thousand requests while also guessing how likely people would be to say yes. Participants significantly underestimated how often people agreed to help, even to morally wrong requests like vandalizing a library book. Go on: ask, and give someone a chance to be happy.

YOU ARE HUMAN WHEN YOU ARE STRUGGLING

Every Friday afternoon, I tidy up my house. I gather up my papers and books, clean the bathroom and the kitchen, dust, and vacuum the floors. When I'm done, the house looks so lovely, clean, and orga-

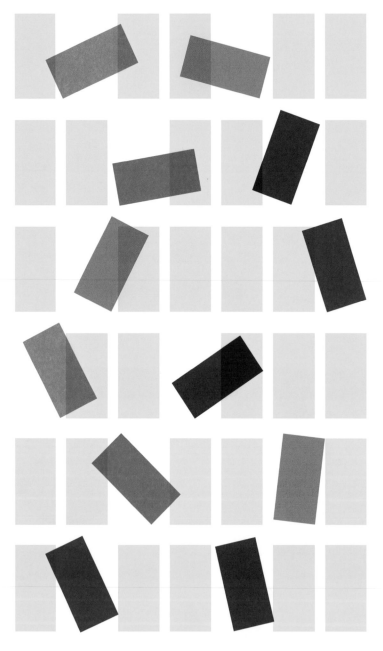

There's no such thing as a happy life that is free of pain.
In every life, there are times of both joy and sorrow.

nized. Every week, I say to myself, "I am going to keep it this tidy forever." And yet, every week, I run into the same problem. I live here. As soon as it's all tidied up, it starts to get messy again.

This is what it's like to be a human. Despite all of the evidence to the contrary, we think that there will be a magical moment when we'll be able to get our life all figured out, and it will stay that way forever.

Old Happy makes it seem like if we can just achieve a certain level of success, our pain will go away. In a 2020 interview, Michael Phelps described how there isn't a finish line or an end point when it comes to happiness. After he won Gold at the Rio Olympics, the media wanted to paint the picture that attending a treatment programme for depression and receiving the gold medal made him all better when in reality it was not that easy.

Twenty-eight Olympic medals won't make you happy. They won't eliminate your suffering, either.

I used to believe that a happy life was one in which you had eliminated all your pain. I now know that a happy life is one in which you live alongside your pain.

Our lives have glorious moments when everything feels bright, shiny, and beautiful: the moments when you fall in love, achieve a dream, or begin a new adventure. But these comprise a mere fraction of your life, and they fade away so quickly.

The rest of the time, you are dealing with some version of a mess: ranging from profound hardship or trauma, all the way to daily struggles like being bored at work, having a rough patch in your marriage, coping with a bad boss, or navigating health problems. Happiness is defined by the way you find joy alongside and after these experiences.

This is what it is like for everyone, no matter how successful they are. The presence of struggles doesn't indicate there is something wrong with you or your life. It just indicates that you are a human being.

It's all too easy to forget this, living in a world that hides pain away, treating it as shameful or as evidence that you're lacking. Even though every single one of us intimately knows what it is like to suffer, open discussion of pain is still so rare.

I'm sure you can recall times where you were struggling but pretended that everything was fine: you pushed your pain way deep down, put on a smile, and said, "I'm good, thanks!" Old Happy culture prioritizes outer appearances over inner well-being, and this ends up hurting all of us. Pain that is hidden away can't be healed, but pain that is faced can.

We shy away from suffering—both our own and others'—misguidedly thinking that this will help us to experience greater happiness. Instead, we need to do the opposite: open up to our pain and meet it with compassion, recognizing that it is an inevitable part of the human experience. Kristin Neff, a psychologist who established the study of self-compassion, calls this "our common humanity." The next time you are struggling, say to yourself: "It's okay to be having a hard time right now. There isn't anything wrong with me. I'm a human being, and this is a part of the human experience."

Consider how you might share your pain with others, too.

The story of the Zimbabwean psychiatrist Dixon Chibanda demonstrates the impact these conversations can have. Several years ago, one of Chibanda's patients died by suicide. They couldn't afford the bus fare to come and see him at his hospital, two hundred miles away from their home. It forced him to reckon with the limitations of his practice. He kept wondering what he could have done to help them.

Then one day he had an idea: within every local community, there are people perfectly suited to supporting others—grandmothers. He gave the grandmothers a month of basic mental health skills training. When they graduated this training, they were given a local bench where they would meet with people to have compassionate conversations about their difficulties.

The program is called Friendship Bench (suggested by one of the grandmothers, who argued that the original name, Mental Health Bench, was stigmatizing). Thousands of grandmothers have now been given their benches, helping more than sixty thousand people in 2022 alone.

Studies of the program show that not only did patients see meaningful mental health improvements, but the grandmothers did, too. Open conversations about pain help us all.

YOU ARE CONNECTED WHEN YOU ARE STRUGGLING

I know that you've been through some hard things in your life. You've been excluded, heartbroken, grieving. You've been ashamed and sorrowful and lonely and scared. Knowing that makes me love you, even though I don't know you.

Think about a hard experience you have been through. How would you describe it to someone else?

"I just lost my father."

"I had a traumatic childhood."

"My spouse and I keep fighting."

"I feel so lost and confused."

"I'm so stressed about paying my bills right now."

"My child is struggling, and I don't know how to help them."

Here's an example from my own life. I used to describe my experience as, "I am a young caregiver for a sick partner who has a mysterious degenerative disease that no doctor understands or can help with."

Thinking about it like that made me so lonely. I didn't know anyone who had been through something similar. That led to me shutting myself off from other people's struggles, thinking my pain was different from theirs. That made me more self-centered and, thus, less able to tap into compassion for myself and others.

One day, I started describing my pain in a new way: "I am a person who has been affected by a devastating illness." I could instantly see so many people in my life who had been through their own versions of this pain—dementia, cancer, heart disease. My overlap expanded, and I was connected to many more people now.

Finally I went even bigger: "I am a person who has gone through pain." Suddenly, *wow*, I'm connected to everyone.

In opening up to ways in which our pain connects us, we are able to tap into another level of compassion for ourselves and others. This makes it possible to do something with it. Connection makes our pain bearable. Who could bear pain if they were alone in this world, with no one to help them through it? Who could bear pain without the potential of transfiguring it through service to another person?

The Spanish philosopher Miguel de Unamuno said that "man dies of cold, not of darkness." It's not the pain that does us in. It's feeling alone in our pain.

That was a key reason that Phelps started talking about his mental health—to help others.

In our shared pain, we discover that we are not alone after all. The darkness may still be there, but the cold has gone.

KEY TAKEAWAYS

- Everyone needs help. Asking for help from another person gives them a chance to experience happiness.

- When you are having a hard time, practice looking at yourself with loving eyes.

- Make a Signal List to identify your signs that you might need to ask someone for help. Consider sharing it with your loved ones.

Everyone suffers. When you remember this, your pain can
become something that connects you to other people.

- There's no magical moment where our lives will be free of suffering. Instead, we need to learn to meet pain with compassion and recognize that it is part of the human experience.

- We can change the way that we look at our pain, from something that isolates us to something that connects us. Look at your own challenges, and consider how they connect you to others.

9

Opportunities for Joy Are Everywhere, If You Know Where to Look

Shigeru Miyamoto, the renowned designer and game director at Nintendo who invented *Mario Bros.*, *Donkey Kong*, and *The Legend of Zelda*, once was asked in an interview what he would do if he could redesign the world.

He answered, "I wish I could make it so that people were more thoughtful and kind toward each other. I wish we were all a little more compassionate in these small ways. If there was a way to design the world that discouraged selfishness, that would be a change I would make."

This is the change that *we* are going to make.

What Miyamoto is describing is a shift from Old Happy's egosystem to New Happy's ecosystem. These terms (which are exquisite, aren't they?) were defined by the psychologists Jennifer Crocker and Amy Canevello.

In an egosystem, a person's core goal is to present themselves in a way that boosts their ego. They pursue their own needs and desires, not caring if they have to use or step on other people along the way because they see life as a competition that they need to win.

In an ecosystem, on the other hand, people recognize that they are a part of a broader web of connections, that what they do affects other people, and that caring for those people contributes to their own happiness.

We can't hand over the design of our world to Miyamoto. We are the designers of our world; it is our power to change it in the way we want it to look. As the designers, we have a specific canvas that we can use: our relationships.

OUR MOMENTS OF CONNECTION

Imagine this. It's an ordinary day. Your alarm goes off. You get out of bed and shuffle to the kitchen. A little while later, your kids wake up, and you get them fed, ready for school, and head out the door.

At work, you spend your day talking with your team and clients. You get a message: your friends want to do a family barbecue on Saturday and wonder if you're in? Time for a quick lunch break down at the food trucks in the local park. You talk to your coworker about how their spouse is feeling after completing a grueling round of chemotherapy treatments. In the afternoon, you head down to the coffee cart to get your favorite drink. Later, you head home to meet your partner, who left work early to take the kids to the playground down the street.

Getting home, you cook dinner from the food you picked up at the market and then FaceTime with Grandma and Grandpa. After the kids are in bed, you turn on the news and hear about some wildfires happening a few hundred miles away. You switch to the television series that everyone's raving about. Then it's off to bed. Another day done.

This is an ordinary day, isn't it? And yet it's not ordinary at all. It's extraordinary.

Each of us are interacting, all day and every day, with our connections. In this ordinary day, you are engaging with all of these:

- Your family
- Your coworkers

- Your clients
- Your friends
- Your community

- Our broader culture
- Nature

What we think of as ordinary daily life is really participating in an ecosystem of giving ourselves to the world and having others give themselves to us in return.

These daily moments of connection are the best place to start living your New Happy. Within them, there are three powerful shifts that you can make.

"HOW CAN I HELP?"

In the early 1990s, the actress Octavia Spencer moved to Los Angeles to try to make it in Hollywood. One day, she was driving to an audition when her car broke down, right in the middle of a busy intersection. Everyone was honking and yelling at her to move her car—which was falling apart and covered in bird droppings—out of the way. But no one helped her.

Then, she heard a motorcycle roar up next to her. A man swung off the seat and said, "Hey, do you need some help?" It was Keanu Reeves. He ushered her into her car and pushed it out of the intersection.

Reeves saw an opportunity to be a helper and took it. You can, too. This is the first shift: "How can I help?"

Think about that ordinary day from earlier. There were a number of moments of connection where you could make this shift:

- With your coworker: After your coworker talked about their spouse's chemotherapy treatments, you could offer to drop off some home-cooked meals.
- With your community: After your friends invited you to the barbecue, you could say yes and ask if you can invite your new neighbors, who just moved to the area and don't know anyone yet.

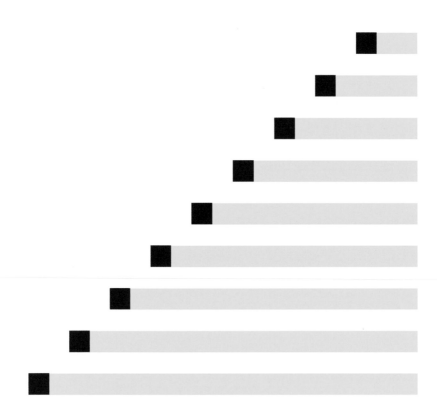

You can start helping right now. As you go through your day, look for opportunities to help another person.

- With the world: After you heard about the local wildfires,
  you could look up a fundraiser and donate a bit of money
  to help.

Studies show that one of the things that prevents us from helping is thinking about ourselves. We get self-conscious: "Will I do a bad job? Will I say the right thing?" Or we worry about the value of our contribution: "Will this even help?" As it turns out, these worries are foolish: if we can get past our fear to offer kindness, people truly and deeply appreciate it.

Émile Durkheim, the founder of sociology, wrote that "altruism is no mere ornament to social life, but its fundamental basis." Every act of care is a stitch, and those stitches are what hold all of us together.

"WHO HELPED ME?"

A friend of mine, Amanda, once told me a story that's always stuck with me. She was rushing to catch her train to work while on an intense work phone call. After parking her car, she grabbed her bag from the trunk and began walking down the long train platform.

She was all the way to the far end of the platform when she realized that she'd been so distracted, she had forgotten to close her trunk. Sighing with frustration and turning back, she saw a stranger passing by her car. They looked around, trying to figure out if someone was coming back. Not seeing anyone, they closed the trunk and kept walking. If Amanda hadn't realized her mistake, she never would have seen that little moment, and she never would have known that she had been the recipient of help.

It's all too easy to take the help we receive for granted. I know that I constantly struggle to remember this. It's why the second shift is so important: "Who helped me?"

In the ordinary day from earlier, you benefitted from others' help, too:

- At work: Your colleague sent you a quick message,
  congratulating you on a great presentation to your clients.

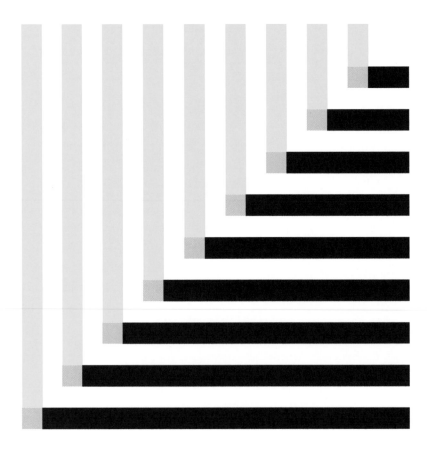

Every day, we receive help that often goes unnoticed.
Look around and see how people are helping you.

- At the coffee cart: The barista had your favorite coffee waiting for you, knowing you always come down at 2:30 p.m. on the dot.
- With your family: Your partner left their work early so that they could pick up the kids and take them to the park, helping you have extra time to finish up your work.

When you pay attention to the help you have benefitted from, it can fill you with an overwhelming sense of gratitude. This, in turn, has been demonstrated to be one of the best contributors to your own happiness and health, with studies documenting improvements to depression, anxiety, blood pressure, and quality of life.

Some researchers describe gratitude as a buffer that protects you against stress. But I don't think it's the gratitude that does it: it's the *people* who have given you the reason for gratitude. You're no longer out there, struggling to do it all on your own. There are people around you, protecting you and nurturing you and helping you. You see that you're not on your own after all. There's a lot to be grateful for when we're no longer separate from one another.

"WHERE ARE OTHERS HELPING?"

Every day, we can open the newspaper and read about people who are hurting other people. Over time, many of us come to believe that the world is a dangerous place, filled with bad people.

This is what's known as a "primal" belief, a term coined by psychologist Jer Clifton of the University of Pennsylvania. It answers the worldview question "Is the world a bad place or a good place?"

Many have argued that it's advantageous to believe the world is dangerous. They say it protects us from life's inevitable suffering, makes us wiser and more rational, and gives us a competitive edge. Those people who believe that the world is a good place are naive at best, but more likely just stupid.

Yet according to Clifton's research, they're wrong. Believing the

Look beyond yourself: people everywhere are helping each other.

world is bad doesn't actually help you achieve positive outcomes like career success, fulfillment, or happiness. In one study, he asked thousands of people what they believed about the world and then reviewed how that worldview has impacted their lives. The people who believed the world was a bad place were . . .

- Less physically and mentally healthy
- More likely to have attempted suicide
- More likely to be dissatisfied at work (and perform slightly below par in their jobs)
- Less likely to be happy

On the other hand, believing that the world was a good place was connected to success, health, and happiness.

If I catch myself feeling cynical, I often remind myself of something that Anne Frank wrote in her diary while hiding from the Nazis in a cramped attic: "In spite of everything, I still believe that people are really good at heart."

This is the third shift. Ask yourself: "Where are others helping?" In that ordinary day, others were helping all around you:

- At home: Your older child taught your younger child a new game while they were playing at the park.
- With your coworker: Their spouse, suffering from cancer, was being treated by highly trained medical professionals, who were doing everything they could to help.
- In the world: The firefighters combating the wildfires were helping protect people, animals, and homes.

Make it a habit to note and share the good you witness others doing: the colleagues who started a fundraiser, the friends who are speaking up for justice, the kid who shares their cookies with your kid at school. Point it out to others, too. Amass the evidence that this is a good world, full of good people.

This belief matters. We model what we see others doing. If you see a world full of people who are only doing things for themselves, how will that change what you do? You will likely act similarly because it's in your best interest to protect yourself. But if you see others behaving generously and kindly, it inspires you to do the same.

Your good actions then become something that influences others. As the author Paulo Coelho wrote, "The world is changed by your example, not your opinion." Every time you do something good in the world, you are providing the evidence to someone else—a reason to keep believing in our collective goodness. If you are ever feeling despair about the world, tell yourself: "I'm going to go be someone's evidence."

When you see someone helping, you feel something deep inside you, like there's a string in your heart that's being strummed: it hums in recognition, seeing that *this* is who we really are.

I felt that strumming when I read about the elderly Japanese group who volunteered to go into the Fukushima nuclear power plant after the 2011 disaster, believing that they should be the ones to face the impacts of radiation. I also felt it when I saw how one of Alex's nurses, Alain, always had his favorite pillow and blanket ready, doing what he could to make him a tiny bit more comfortable.

When our hearts are strummed, something wonderful happens. Studies have found that just witnessing someone be kind makes *you* more likely to be kind to others, too. It sparks a response, a desire to contribute. If you follow through, it will spread far beyond you because helping is contagious and spreads through communities.

Every time you help, you're not just doing one good thing. You're kicking off a chain reaction of many good things. Your strumming heart can inspire the swelling symphony of a whole orchestra.

THE BIGGEST SHIFT YOU CAN MAKE

These three daily shifts—"How can I help?" "Who helped me?" and "Where are others helping?"—have the power to make you and others happier, every single day.

It's also possible to unlock an even deeper, greater form of happiness by choosing to craft a life in which we integrate helping into all that we do.

In the 1980s, the world was on edge due to Cold War tension and devastation from the Ethiopian famine. A group of social scientists was trying to figure out what they could do to help. Among them were Stanford psychologists William Damon and Anne Colby.

Damon and Colby wondered what they might learn if they studied moral exemplars—heroes like Martin Luther King Jr., Nelson Mandela, Florence Nightingale, and Sojourner Truth. Were they born with their values, or did a life event shape them? What sets them apart from the rest of us? And most importantly, could their pathways be taught to others in order to inspire moral behavior?

To answer these questions, Damon and Colby decided to launch a study that looked at ordinary people who did extraordinary things to help others. After coming up with a highly selective list of criteria, they identified twenty-two people to interview.

From the outside, these people appeared to have nothing in common. Some of them had PhDs, while others had never graduated high school. There were business executives and nonprofit employees. Some worked in religious organizations, while others worked in the media. Their ages spanned more than fifty years, from thirty-five to eighty-six. Some came from wealth, and others had grown up in poverty. They held a range of political views and cared about different causes.

As Damon and Colby dug deeper, though, they discovered that these extraordinary people shared several key qualities.

They had a sense of certainty: they knew what was right and what was wrong, and they felt a responsibility to take action in alignment with those beliefs.

They also experienced profound joy in their daily lives and felt optimistic about the future. A lot of people tend to think that living in service means either that you will be living a dull, boring life, empty of pleasure, or that you will be overwhelmed with the suffering you're trying to address. This shows us that neither is true. Service increases your hope and happiness.

But most importantly, they did not see their personal goals and their goals for the world as separate or at odds. They were the same thing, intertwined and reinforcing one another. They could work toward their own happiness and the happiness of the world at the same time.

This is what Abraham Maslow independently realized, too, upon discovering that he'd forgotten the sixth need, for self-transcendence. He described how he had gotten it all wrong: the people he studied who were 'self actualizing' were only able to do so because they were devoted to the needs of others. The two were not separate: they were intertwined. Self-actualizing people care deeply about other people's well-being, seek to improve the world, fight for justice in all of its forms, and strive to embody compassion in all that they do. The best helpers, Maslow wrote, were also the most 'fully human' people. The truth was suddenly so clear: the best way to be of service to others is to become who you are capable of being; but in order to do that, you have to help people. You have to pursue both.

Here, again, are the two threads—being yourself and giving of yourself—but now, brought together, achieved simultaneously.

This is the final shift, the big one: craft a life in which you can be yourself and give of yourself at the same time. You do this by using your gifts to serve the world.

In Mary Oliver's poem "Song of the Builders," she describes sitting on a hill and watching a cricket slowly breaking down organic matter. That's the cricket's unique role in our ecosystem, and the whole world relies on it to bring those nutrients back into the earth. Oliver implores us to remember that we all have our own "inexplicable way" to contribute to the world around us.

You, too, have your own role, one that uses your unique gifts—all that you are, know, and do. In the coming chapters, you'll discover those gifts and how to start using them.

KEY TAKEAWAYS

- Start seeing yourself as a designer of our world. Your actions can change the world from an egosystem to an ecosystem.

- The first shift is, "How can I help?" Look for ways to contribute.

- The second shift is, "Who helped me?" Pay attention to moments of support that benefit you.

- The third shift is, "Where are others helping?" Amass the evidence that we live in a good world.

- The final shift is to weave helping into your life by using your gifts to serve the world. This allows you to self-actualize and self-transcend at the same time.

PART FOUR

Uncover Your Gifts

10

Why You Matter

"Daddy, tell me a story."

These words are familiar to every parent. But for Richard Adams, they were words that changed his life.

The request came one day as he drove his daughters to school. He started making up a story on the spot, the tale of two rabbits named Hazel and Fiver who were forced to go on a dangerous journey in order to find a new place to live, facing great evil along the way. His daughters were riveted and begged him to write it down, eventually bothering him so much that he caved.

Adams had never written fiction before—his whole life had been spent working for the UK's Civil Service. But after months of writing in the evenings, he completed his manuscript. It was rejected seven times before a small publisher agreed to take it on, only printing two thousand copies.

This book was *Watership Down*, one of the most successful and beloved children's books of all time. It won the Andrew Carnegie Medal, one of the most prestigious fiction awards, and sold millions of copies. For a time, it even became Penguin's best-selling book ever.

Richard Adams, at the age of fifty-two, had discovered his gifts.

THE THREE TYPES OF GIFTS

The Roman Catholic monk Thomas Merton once wrote, "Every man

Within each of us are the gifts of humanity, talent, and wisdom.

has a vocation to be someone: but he must understand clearly that in order to fulfill this vocation he can only be one person: himself."

How do you discover what makes you *you*? Many people during the years have offered their own answers to this question. I've been lucky enough to learn from many. My training in positive psychology taught me to look at human beings, based not on what we lack, but on our strengths. Psychologists Martin Seligman and Christopher Peterson proposed that our inner character is good and can be cultivated, and that we all have unique strengths that can transform our well-being and our lives. Another founder of the field, Mihaly Csikszentmihalyi, devoted much of his career to the study of human potential, talent, and mastery. I built upon all of their contributions by conducting extensive research in different fields, including philosophy, religious studies, and the arts, as well as interviewing people living New Happy lives to identify what qualities they shared.

Every human being possesses three gifts: humanity, talent, and wisdom. They are all grounded in the New Happy worldview:

- They begin within your true self.
- They are cultivated and expressed outwardly through action.
- They contribute to well-being for you and for the world at the same time.

Using Richard Adams's story, let's explore each of the three gifts. The first type of gift is your humanity—who you are.

Your humanity is the way that you share your true self's inner goodness. In Adams's case, his humanity was expressed through the way that *Watership Down* teaches us something important about who we are and how we can better treat one another and the world.

Although Adams insisted that the book was not a parable or a moral teaching, readers have pointed out key lessons that he included in the book: a rebuke of the way we treat nature and animals, the dangers of unchecked power, and how politics affects everyday life.

And of course, Adams's gift was sparked by his love for his children. Without them, he never would have written the book.

The second type of gift is your talent—what you do.

Watership Down is a scary book, and Adams had a talent for both tolerating scary things and sharing them with others. He remembered reading frightening books as a child, crying in fear but unable to tear himself away from the pages. His children were often so terrified by his bedtime stories that they were not able to sleep through the night.

Adams was a natural storyteller and often entertained his daughters. He turned that storytelling gift into a talent for writing, publishing more than fifteen books during the course of his life after *Watership Down*.

The third type of gift is your wisdom—what you know.

Watership Down plucked insights from Adams's time in the military, his homeland of Hampshire, and what he knew about wildlife creatures and wove it all together in a tale that kept his daughters (and millions of readers) terrified—and riveted.

His deepest piece of wisdom was that, contrary to popular opinion, children could handle scary stories and deeper, more meaningful messages. He felt that too many authors and publishers talked down to children and tried to hide the reality of the world from them, denying them essential messages about life and the world along the way. He knew that art was for telling the truth, no matter the audience.

EXPERIENCE JOY THAT BUILDS

There's an easy way to know if you have discovered one of your gifts: using it will make you feel good.

You are allowed to feel good. You know that, right? It is so important that you realize that. Your gifts should bring you joy. When you use your gifts, you feel connected to your true self; you feel alive and energized. Gifts will whisper to you, "This is what I'm supposed to be doing."

In an interview with *The Paris Review*, the Nobel and Pulitzer Prize–winning author Toni Morrison was describing her passion for politics. The interviewer asked her why she didn't do that as her work instead of writing. "I don't think that I could show up on a regular basis as a politician," she replied. "I would lose interest. I don't have the resources for it, the gift. There are people who can organize other people and I cannot. I'd just get bored."

In fact, it took Morrison a while to figure out that writing was her true gift. She was frequently praised for her writing abilities, but she had to turn within to recognize that writing made her feel alive and gave her a sense of purpose. No one else can tell you what your gifts are. You will know based on how it feels to you.

The joy of discovering your gifts will expand when you combine them all together into something that is utterly irreplicable. Consider Richard Adams. There are other writers. There are other fathers who tell scary stories. There are other people living in Hampshire. There are other people who fought in the war. But there was no one else who had the unique combination of gifts that led him to write *Watership Down*.

Gifts are incomparable because they do not operate in isolation. It's the way that they come together, like a tapestry woven of different-colored strings, that makes them completely unique.

In Old Happy culture, we use comparison to define our success and measure our worth. But no one else has the same combination of gifts that you do, your special blend of humanity, talent, and wisdom. You are one of one, surrounded by other people who are all one of one, too.

Finally, your joy expands even further when you use your incomparable gifts to make a contribution to others.

All of these things that you do, know, and are—they have a purpose: to be given away. Why else are we endowed with this humanity, these talents, this wisdom? As the author Annie Dillard wrote, "Anything you do not give freely and abundantly becomes lost to you. You open your safe and find ashes."

And as we have seen, using your gifts solely for extrinsic ends doesn't work, either. They need to be offered to another; that's why they're called gifts.

In the next three chapters, we're going to deep dive into each gift, covering the strategies and tools that help you discover and start to use your own. To help, I have created an interactive workbook that you can use as you go through these chapters, available at thenewhappy.com/resources.

HOW TO CELEBRATE OTHER PEOPLE'S GIFTS

One surprising way to discover your gifts is to start looking for them in other people. Seeing another person use a gift familiarizes you with it, making it easier for you to spot that gift in yourself, too.

To do this, we want to take our cue from the legendary sculptor Michelangelo, who allegedly said that his job was to release the hidden figure from the raw block of marble in front of him.

Michelangelo argues that the person within the block of marble is already fully formed, truly and authentically themselves, but unable to burst through what is in their way. As the sculptor, he has one job: removing the barriers that are impeding their freedom. Scientists now call this the "Michelangelo phenomenon": it turns out that supportive relationships have the power to help you become more and more yourself.

We don't need to use a mallet and a chisel to help our loved ones find their gifts. Instead, we want to be a mirror, a strategy first proposed by Aristotle.

A friend of mine named Cory has a job in which she onboards new employees to her company. A few of her gifts include facilitating, teaching, and igniting enthusiasm in others. I noticed her using these gifts outside of work, and I pointed it out:

- She created a book club that she facilitates every week.

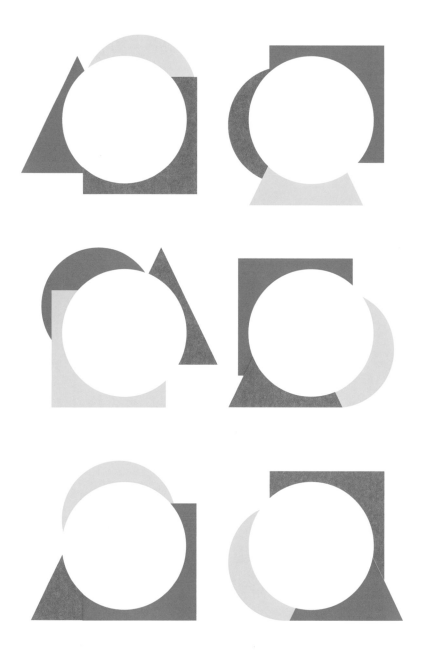

Look for other people's gifts and point them out whenever you can.
It will show you the many different ways that gifts can manifest.

- After deciding to freeze her eggs, she documented it on social media so others could learn from her experience.
- She does yearly charity challenges to raise money for causes that affect her loved ones, rallying a group of friends to join in.

Cory was shocked. She didn't know these were her gifts, let alone how frequently she was using them. With this new knowledge, she can make decisions that help her use these gifts more frequently; for example, she recently started giving free monthly mentoring sessions to people who have lost their jobs.

What are other people good at? When you see something, reflect it to them through a specific compliment.

Humanity:
- "You're incredible at staying calm when the restaurant is so busy."
- "I appreciate how you always check in with me and ask how I'm feeling."
- "I was inspired by the way you listened to that customer's needs and got their returns all sorted out."

Talent:
- "I am grateful that you kept the project on time and on budget. Thank you for your diligent planning."
- "Will you show me more of your writing?"
- "I love seeing you standing up on that stage. You shine when you tell stories."

Wisdom:
- "I've never thought about this situation in that way."
- "Thank you for pointing out that issue. Your expertise is really helpful."

- "I was really struggling with knowing what to do next, but I wanted to let you know that it helped me so much to hear how you solved a similar problem in the past."

No one's gifts can emerge and develop without another person there to identify, nurture, and encourage them. If you were alone, with no family, friends, teachers, classes, collaborators, role models, and inspiration, how could you ever discover and use your gifts?

Ryan Coogler, the writer and director of the Academy Award–winning and beloved movie *Black Panther*, got into writing because of a college professor's mirroring. He was a college football player and, as part of the curriculum, had to take a creative writing class. In one session, the professor asked the students to write about their most intense, emotional life experience. A few days later, she called Coogler into her office. He thought he was in trouble, but in fact, she wanted to tell him how good his piece was and particularly how visually striking she thought it was. She encouraged him to think about writing screenplays. That single comment propelled Coogler into a career that has made such a positive impact on the world.

When I think back on my own life, I feel that I owe everything to my mirrors: my second-grade teacher, Mary Bloch, who read my first "book" and encouraged me to keep writing; my high-school art teacher, Marg Hagey, who let me hang out in the studio making abstract art; and my parents, who encouraged my passions for the big questions in life and did everything they could to help me investigate them. Without these people, I wouldn't be writing these words. They were the mirrors that helped me see myself.

THE IMPACT YOUR GIFTS WILL MAKE

Darren O'Brien is a rail station manager in England, working for Southeastern Railways. One night, he saw a Channel 4 documentary that told the stories of women escaping abusive partners. On the screen, he saw a woman and her children who were trying to get to a

By sharing your unique combination of gifts, you will create new
connections with others and make a difference in the world.

safe place but were unable to do so because of the cost of the train tickets. It's incredibly difficult to escape abusers, in part because they tend to control their victim's finances.

As O'Brien told me, when the documentary ended, he turned to his wife and said, "I'm going to do something about this." The next day at work, he went to his boss and proposed a solution: what if Southeastern offered anyone escaping domestic violence a secure, undetectable way to get a free train ticket?

After a lot of work from O'Brien, the program was approved and Southeastern launched the Rails to Refuge program. The initiative offers anyone escaping a violent partner a free, untraceable ticket sent to their mobile phone.

When the pandemic hit, the United Kingdom experienced a 60 percent increase in calls to domestic abuse hotlines. Southeastern persuaded other railways across the country to join the program, making it possible to travel anywhere in the United Kingdom using Rails to Refuge. O'Brien told me he's now working to try to get ferries on board so that people on remote islands can get to safety, too. His greatest dream is that transport systems around the world will create similar programs.

O'Brien had humanity: he wanted to help the people he saw suffering. He had wisdom: he realized that railways could make it easier for survivors to flee. And he had talents: he proposed and advocated for the program within Southeastern to make it a reality. He brought them all together to help in a way that only he could.

But his gifts did not stand alone; they would never have been sparked were it not for the woman who courageously starred in the documentary he saw. She was a domestic violence survivor herself. After she escaped, she used her own gifts to help others trapped in similar situations and eventually became the CEO of a refuge.

The documentary starring many brave survivors was made by a group of filmmakers who used their gifts to tell the story in such a powerful way that it affected O'Brien. (In turn, it was aired on a television channel that required thousands of peoples' gifts to stay up and running, and so on . . .)

The Rails to Refuge program has now saved more than three thousand people and continues to transport four people to safety every day.

When this woman was escaping her abuser thirty years ago, doing the courageous and difficult work of healing from her experiences, could she ever have imagined the impact that her individual act of courage would have, the ripple effects that will unfold outward over the next few generations?

This is how gifts work. They take what is within you and extend it outward, lifting and enlivening all of those who are touched by them—and they spark the same impulse within others. As O'Brien said to me, "I think it's our job to do good in life where we can for others, who then might do the same in their own ways. Suddenly, we found that we've built a community of people who are changing the world."

As we use our gifts, we are slowly forging a chain, adding a new link every time one is used. We don't know where it might lead, what it might connect to, or who will use it.

Occasionally, we get to witness glimpses of the chain, and they remind us of what matters most. O'Brien told me that one of the most moving moments of his life was meeting some of the survivors who had used the Rails to Refuge program, including a woman who had escaped while pregnant.

Sometimes your job is to be the unseen link in the chain. You don't know it, but you are connecting one person to another person who needs them. Those Channel 4 documentarians, broadcasters, technicians, and producers might not even know that their daily work directly led to helping three thousand people find safety. What they took for granted as an ordinary day was, in fact, a day of heroism.

And sometimes you're the person who pulls on the chain and you are lifted up at the moment you need it most.

Every time you use your gifts, you're acting with faith that you are a part of the chain, that what you do matters and adds up. We each contribute our little bit, trusting that we are collectively creating something wonderful: a world where we can better care for one another.

KEY TAKEAWAYS

- Everyone has gifts. There are three types: humanity, talent, and wisdom.

- Gifts are joyful, incomparable, and make a contribution to others.

- Help someone else find their gifts by acting as their mirror, pointing out what they're good at.

- Using your gifts connects you to other people in another way.

11

Humanity:
The Foundation
for Everything We Do

In 2013, Shiro Oguni, a television presenter in Japan, was brought the wrong lunch order while dining in a restaurant for a story. Instead of a hamburger, he received *gyoza*, or pan-fried dumplings. But he wasn't eating in a normal restaurant. He was visiting a dementia care home, an atypical one where patients did their own cooking and cleaning and even ran the café together.

Looking at his plate, Oguni realized it wasn't a big deal that they got his order wrong. Mistakes happen. What was a big deal was that these people, so often abandoned by society, were being treated like human beings. "Calling someone 'The demented Mrs. Whozit' is completely different from 'Mrs. Whozit with dementia,'" he asserted. "People are people. The change will not come from them, it must come from society. By cultivating tolerance, almost anything can be solved."

He decided he wanted to help change the way society treated people with dementia. Several years later, he opened The Restaurant of Mistaken Orders. As he described it, "The restaurant is not about whether orders are executed incorrectly or not. The important thing is the interaction with people who have dementia." Oguni surveyed diners as they left the restaurant: 37 percent of orders were incorrect, yet 99 percent of customers were satisfied.

The restaurant was a huge hit, starting a conversation about different ways society could better support those with dementia. It even won one of the world's highest creative awards, the Cannes Lion. Most important, the staff experienced a profound shift in their well-being and were often seen beaming with joy as they served patrons. Oguni was right about how important this connection was: one recent study found that people with dementia who have just one hour of connection every week experience a significant increase in their quality of life.

WE HAVE GOTTEN LOVE ALL WRONG

In Oguni's story, we can see the first type of gift at work: humanity.

Humanity is the only type of gift that is required for happiness. It's the foundation upon which we build our talent and wisdom, as we see in Oguni's story. He combined his humanity gift (extending compassion to people with dementia) with his wisdom gift (we can make a space where it's okay for people with dementia to make mistakes) with his talent gift (creating experiences that start conversations).

Back in chapter 4, you learned about your true self and its good, loving nature. Your humanity gifts are the way you express that love.

Our culture portrays love as something that's confined to a romantic relationship, a dramatic and passionate roller coaster that fades to black as a title card reads, "And they lived happily ever after."

But according to the latest research led by Barbara Fredrickson of the University of North Carolina at Chapel Hill, love is something quite different: it's an emotion, shared between two people, that results in a desire to invest in each other's well-being. This emotion can be experienced with anyone—not just your partner or kids, but with a friend, a coworker, or even a stranger.

To share love with another is, in fact, one of the most powerful things that you can do for your own well-being. Imagine that there was a pill you could take that would make you instantly healthier. It's associated with lower blood pressure, improved heart health, reduced stress, and less depression. It strengthens your relationships, makes you more resilient, increases your sense of meaning in life, and helps your mental health. On top of those incredible benefits, the pill doesn't cost any money or have any negative side effects. People would be begging their doctors for a prescription.

That pill exists, and it is called love.

Each of us has a nerve that connects the brain to the heart, known as the vagus nerve. This nerve is part of our bodies that helps us experience love. Researchers can measure how "strong" this nerve is, resulting in a measurement called the vagal tone. Think of the vagal tone as a love barometer, showing how loved you're feeling or how loving you're being.

Your vagus nerve kicks into gear when you share a moment of care with another person: laughing over something silly with your kids, helping a colleague on a project, talking about your day with a friend, or having a nice chat with a cashier at the grocery store. You start mimicking each other, smiling and moving in similar ways. Your autonomic nervous system and neural firing start to align with the other person's. You're filled with a desire to contribute to this person's life, to make them happy. That's love—real love.

When you feel and follow through on that loving feeling, and do something to help another person, you are using your humanity gifts.

This takes so many different forms: Kindness. Compassion. Courage. Forgiveness. Patience. Encouragement. Comfort. Interest. Appreciation. Empowerment. Celebration. Playfulness. Empathy. Tenderness. Care. Presence. Tolerance. Curiosity. Mutuality. Acceptance. Generosity. Openness. Understanding. Delight. All of these actions fall under the banner of humanity gifts.

You might be thinking to yourself, "*These* are my humanity gifts? Isn't this just normal human behavior?"

It's true that we were physically made to love. Beginning with our ancestors, we have evolved to depend fiercely on one another. Human beings have the longest developmental period of any animal in the world, and without a sustained, loving bond to others, we would not survive. This was proven in an evil experiment. In the thirteenth century, Emperor Frederick II wanted to figure out what the "inborn language of mankind" was. He ordered a group of children to be raised in seclusion, where they would never hear any form of speech. The babies were physically cared for but never spoken to, played with, or loved. Before he could discover the inborn language, all of the babies had died.

Our humanity gifts have not been valued by society, even though, without them, there would be no society at all. This has impoverished us. We have missed the chance to cultivate them and take them to the great heights that are possible.

Some people are naturally skilled at using their humanity gifts. The rest of us need a little bit of help.

START BY GENERATING LOVE
WITHIN YOU

Picture this: It's dark out, and you're looking at a house at the end of a long lane. All of the curtains are shut. Then, suddenly, someone inside of the house draws back all the curtains. Light floods out through the windows. That's what it looks like to discover your humanity gifts. The light was on the whole time; you just needed to pull back the curtains to let the light shine through.

That's your inner loving nature—something that is accessible to you at any moment in time. One of the best ways to draw the curtains back is a practice called loving-kindness meditation.

This is a Buddhist practice that is designed to cultivate a more compassionate version of ourselves. To do it, you generate loving feelings while repeating a mantra, either out loud or in your head: "May you feel safe and protected. May you feel happy and peaceful. May you feel healthy and strong. May you live with ease." First, you offer it to yourself, then to someone you love, then to someone you're neutral

Every interaction with another person is
a chance to cultivate love within you.

about, and finally, someone you struggle with. At the end, you offer it to all beings everywhere.

In one randomized control trial, researchers taught this meditation technique to a group of people. For nine weeks, each participant meditated for about ten minutes every day. The practice not only increased their ability to generate love for others, but also improved their personal happiness.

You can practice this meditation formally, but I have a specific twist on it that effortlessly integrates it into your daily life. Whenever you pass someone on the streets, at the shops, or at work, look at them for a moment and mentally say, "I hope you will be happy today," or "You deserve love and happiness." Create these pockets of love in every day.

After you have generated these loving emotions within you, it's time to express it. Remember, that's what makes it a gift: love starts within you but must be shared outside of you.

TAKE THE NEXT LOVING ACTION

Kenyan long-distance runner Abel Mutai was about to win the three-thousand-meter race. He was approaching the end of the course, with Spanish runner Iván Fernández Anaya far behind in second place. Suddenly, Mutai stopped short, ten meters before the finish line. He had made a grave error—he thought he had already crossed the line.

Fernández Anaya easily could have overtaken Mutai and taken advantage of his mistake to win. But when he caught up to Mutai, he slowed down, told him to go ahead, and guided him toward the end, staying behind him the whole way.

Overtaking Mutai would have gotten him the glory. But in that moment, Fernández Anaya clearly saw that it wasn't about doing whatever it took to win. It was a moment to do the right thing for another human.

When you slow down—both literally and figuratively—you start to see the opportunities for love that are all around you. A simple

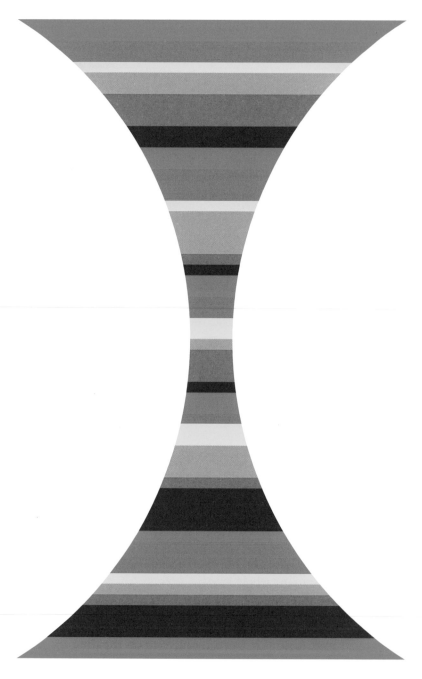

Take the love that is within you and turn it
into actions that help other people.

pause can make all the difference. As you're going about your day, slow down for just a moment and ask yourself: "What would it look like to use my humanity gifts right now?"

There's a famous study from the 1970s that was led by C. Daniel Batson and John Darley of Princeton University. The social psychologists recruited a group of seminary students to prepare a talk on the Good Samaritan, a biblical story describing a kind person helping someone lying on the side of the road in pain. The seminary students were brought to one building, where they took a brief assessment. The students were told that they would have to cross the campus to another building to deliver their speech about the parable. Half of the students were informed that they were running late and needed to hurry; the other half were told they had enough time but should get going.

Unbeknownst to the students, the researchers had asked a team member to lie on the path that ran between the two buildings, slumped over, clearly unwell, and moaning—directly mimicking the conditions of the Good Samaritan parable.

Only 40 percent of the students offered help to the victim. The more rushed and hurried the students were, the less likely they were to stop and help. Of the group of students who were told they were running late, only 10 percent stopped.

These people weren't malicious or callous; when they arrived at the second location, the researchers saw they were flustered about something. Rushing can make us ignore or deprioritize moments of connection. Sometimes it seems like our world is designed to keep us from love.

We can't just accept that this is the way it is. To do so would be to accept an unhappy world. Sometimes you'll run late or catch yourself breezing past someone who needs help. In those moments, come back to this objective: "I will do my best not to rush because when I do, I miss out on the moments of love that are in front of me."

Remember, there's no outcome waiting for us. Where are we rushing to then? This is our life, right here and now. This person in front of us, who needs help, is an opportunity to use our humanity gifts and experience happiness.

Many years ago, I was talking about this with a friend, and he told me about something his dad used to say to him. "Don't forget to look up, Adam," he'd counsel him. Pause—from your phone, your computer, your work, your stress, your tasks, your strivings—and look up. There are people to love right in front of you.

In Alcoholics Anonymous, there's a saying: do the next right thing. For someone trying to stay sober, it can be impossible to imagine a whole life stretching out in front of you in which you can never drink again. But when you shift your focus from the long term to the short term (the next hour or the next day), it becomes much more achievable. You can do the next right thing—not drinking, *today.*

Similarly, it can be overwhelming to ponder how to be a loving person for the rest of your life. It's far more achievable to focus on taking the next loving action. The more we do this, the stronger our loving self becomes, like a muscle we build through action.

We are all constantly benefitting from other people's choices to take the next loving action. Here are a few examples from our community:

- Kindness: "When I was depressed, my friend baked my favorite cookies and left them on my front porch with a card."
- Compassion: "My partner listened to me and supported me as I cried about my family difficulties."
- Forgiveness: "I made a huge mistake at work. My boss was so kind about it and helped me fix it."
- Generosity: "A friend gave me a place to stay when I was homeless."
- Courage: "My friend walked me to a scary doctor's appointment and held my hand in the waiting room."

"Take the next loving action" is also a reminder to pause and discern what love would look like in *this* moment. You have a lot of different humanity gifts that you can draw upon. Which is going to be the most helpful for the person in front of you?

In my research, I spoke to a woman named Julia who told me about her experience with severe postpartum depression. She hadn't slept in days, was in complete despair, and was battling suicidal ideation. Her mom would come over and try to help by cleaning her house. But Julia didn't care about the house. She just wanted someone to give her a brief break from her kids so she could sleep.

Then one of Julia's friends came over. She asked some careful questions, listened, and then told Julia, "You're going to lie on this couch and close your eyes, I'm going to put a towel over your eyes, and you're going to sleep. I'm going to sit next to you and hold your feet. I'll squeeze them if the babies need you. You're going to rest, and I'm going to make sure everything is okay." Julia did as her friend suggested and was able to get her first bit of sleep in days.

Julia's friend's humanity gifts made this moment possible. She took the time to slow down and discern what the problem was, which helped her take the next *right* loving action.

HOW TO STAY OPEN TO LOVE

Rosie Torres was exhausted. In 2008, her husband, Le Roy, had come home from his military tour in Iraq incredibly sick. He had been exposed to his base's burn pit, a ten-acre field where the military doused trash and human waste in oil and then set it on fire, spreading toxic fumes around the base and surrounding area. After more than four hundred doctor visits, Le Roy was diagnosed with the debilitating lung disease constrictive bronchiolitis and a brain injury. The U.S. Department of Veterans Affairs denied his health benefits, he lost his job, and he was suffering from profound depression.

For years, Rosie and Le Roy had been working to try to raise awareness and help the hundreds of thousands of other veterans who had been made ill by the burn pits. They founded an organization called Burn Pits 360 to build community and support one another through

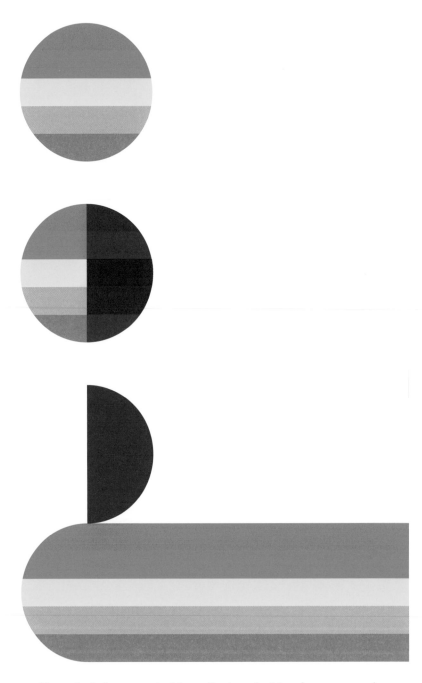

If you feel disconnected from the love inside of you, remember
that it's still there. You can always open back up and share it.

the challenges. They went to Washington, DC, pleading for someone in government to do something, anything, to help those suffering.

Then one day, Rosie saw the comedian Jon Stewart advocating for health care for 9/11 first responders, many of whom were suffering from similar ill-health due to toxic fumes. She approached him: Could he help their cause? It took less than five seconds for him to say yes.

Four years later, Congress passed the Honoring our PACT Act, providing health-care benefits to all those affected by the military's burn pits and other toxic agents.

On the steps of the Capitol, celebrating the victory, Stewart affirmed those who brought him to the cause: "Rosie is the reason I'm doing it, her and Le Roy." Turning to Le Roy, he said, "My brother . . . I talked to Le Roy four years ago in my office and I made a promise to him. I said, 'I'm not gonna let you go, my brother' and 'We're gonna get this done.' And guess what? We got it done. I love you, Le Roy."

Part of using your humanity gifts is staying open to being moved by another person's needs. Stewart was open to overlapping with Rosie, leading to his instant, "Yes, I will help." You also might have experienced this in the past: you see someone struggling and suddenly feel that they are a part of you and that you need to help them.

This is an emotion called *kama muta*, a phrase that comes from Sanskrit and means "moved by love." The anthropologist Alan Page Fiske calls it the "sudden devotion emotion." Many positive viral videos—soldiers coming home to their families, communities coming together, an act of generosity—invoke it.

This small emotion is mighty because it reminds you of how similar you are to others, creating an instant overlap. One study asked participants to watch a heartwarming video sharing the stories of people who were not in their in-group. Watching that video humanized these "others" and made it possible to feel empathy for them. Being moved can help us fight against injustice and address the suffering in the world.

As humans, it's not possible for us to stay in a loving state all of the time. It doesn't matter how often you slip out of love. What matters is how often you come back to it.

There's a tool you can use to help with this that I call "pulling back the curtains." Recall the image of the house in the night, flooded with light. When you slip out of your loving state, it means that the curtains have been drawn closed. Take a breath, and as you do, imagine pulling back the curtains. Be willing to feel love again and then be willing to take the next right loving action.

WHY HUMANITY GIFTS CAN CHANGE THE WORLD

You might believe that your humanity gifts are insignificant amid the trillions of events happening every day in our vast world. Yet they are a tremendous force for good.

Scholars who study peace have identified several major factors that contribute to peaceful societies, many of which are harder to influence, like governments, public health, equality, and economic policies.

But they found something surprising, too, something that is completely within our control. Peaceful societies have many more micro-moments of love shared among their members. These people use their gift of humanity far more frequently. As the lead researchers Peter T. Coleman and Douglas Fry describe it, "Sustaining peace happens through positive reciprocity: I show you a kindness and you do me a favor in return, multiplied throughout the social world a million times over."

It turns out that love really does add up.

KEY TAKEAWAYS

- Your gifts of humanity are the way you express your good, loving nature.

- Start by generating love within you. You can either imagine sending love to someone or mentally do so during your in-person interactions.

- Translate that loving feeling into action by slowing down and asking, "What's the next right loving action?"

- When you realize that you are disconnected from your humanity, remind yourself to open back up the curtains.

- Humanity gifts contribute to a happier, more peaceful world.

12

Talent:
The Invisible Path
to Greatness

When you think of a talented person, who comes to mind? It's probably someone like these folks:

- Leonardo da Vinci, the painter and inventor
- Ada Lovelace, the first computer programmer
- Charles Dickens, the author of many acclaimed novels
- Julia Child, the chef who brought French cooking to America
- Hayao Miyazaki, the animator and cofounder of Studio Ghibli
- Serena Williams, the winner of twenty-three Grand Slams
- Satya Nadella, the CEO of Microsoft

Our world is full of people with diverse talents that awe and inspire. They have reached heights of mastery that seem so far out of reach for the rest of us. It feels unimaginable that they were once a person just like you and me—someone who is confused about what they want, who doesn't know what they're good at, who feels like an imposter.

We don't see their journey of *becoming* those talented selves, which keeps the process shrouded in mystery and very, very hard to replicate for ourselves.

What we do see is an image that reinforces Old Happy. It seems like talent springs forth from these people, perfectly formed. (Hello, perfect self.) Talented people have achieved so many extrinsic goals, like wealth and fame. (Hello, outcomes.) And talents are reserved for just the few brilliant geniuses. (Hello, separation!)

Yet every single one of these people—and many more besides— walked the same invisible path. They got lucky and stumbled upon it, but the rest of us deserve to find it, too.

THE THREE STEPS FOR DISCOVERING YOUR TALENT

More than twenty-four hundred years ago, Aristotle wrote a treatise called *The Nicomachean Ethics*, which continues to shape the fields of philosophy and psychology to this very day. In it, he argues that every person has a "daimon," which is his word for the true self.

Your daimon is where your innate potential lives. Aristotle argued that your task, as a human, is to actualize that inner potential, to bring it forth so that you can become your most *you* self.

We have already explored how to bring forth the love that is within you. Now, it's time to bring forth the potential that is within you. Combining Aristotle's insights with modern research, I've broken it into three steps:

1. Discover your true self's innate potential.
2. Turn your potential into a talent.
3. Evolve your talent over time.

This is the invisible path, now made visible.

STEP #1:
DISCOVER YOUR POTENTIAL

Julia Child had never cared about food. That all changed when her new gastronome husband, Paul, took her to the oldest restaurant in France, La Couronne (operating since 1345!).

There, she sat down and ate a meal that changed her life: a half dozen oysters on the shell, sole meunière in a brown butter sauce, a lightly dressed crisp green salad, and the creamy cheese known as fromage blanc. She later told *The New York Times* that this meal was "an opening up of the soul and spirit for me."

This is how we discover our talents: by paying attention to the feelings that our true self gives us. These feelings might be spiritual in nature, like Child's, or they might be something more subtle, like warmth or calm. They could be a motivation to action, like, "I need to learn more about this," or "I want to try that!" They might be thoughts like, "I wonder . . ." or "That sounds cool!"

Start making a list (or use our workbook, mentioned in chapter 10) where you note these moments in your daily life. This is your "potential list."

It's like you're panning for gold, with your feelings serving as the alert that you've found something worth exploring.

For example, if you're a college student, look for fragments of gold in your classes. Perhaps it's when your professor says something that makes you sit up a little straighter or an offhand reference in a textbook that sends you down a research spiral. You might feel it when you're working with a team on a class project, organizing everyone's efforts to achieve a goal. Or you could be captivated by a guest speaker sharing their career journey.

If you're having trouble, here are a few additional strategies that can help.

Go Back in Time

What did your seven-year-old self love? What subject in school, game, book, or movie? Even if it seems impractical, make a note of it.

To uncover your talents, try as many different things as you can.
When you feel a spark, that's a sign to explore it more deeply.

Steal a Schedule

Who has the day-to-day life that excites you the most? This is the person you look at and think, "Wow, I can't believe they get to wake up every morning and do *that*."

Look for Ease

Is there something that other people struggle with that comes easily to you? Is there something that you enjoy doing that most other people dislike doing?

Ask for Feedback

Make a list of five to ten people who have witnessed you in action, whether at school, at a job, at home, or with your community. Ask them, "What do you think my unique talents are?" or "When have you seen me most alive?" Try to get them to reflect your gifts to you, the way you have learned to do for others.

Avoid asking questions like, "What job do you think I should pursue?" Many people will jump straight to solutions, or how *they* think you should fulfill your potential. But that's your job. You need to filter their answers through your own feelings, asking yourself, "Does this feel right to me?"

If you don't find any gold fragments while panning in your current life, you need to move to a new spot.

Julia Child didn't discover her love for food until she was nearly forty, simply because she hadn't been exposed to the right experience. You need something to spark you, the way a match needs a surface to catch alight.

Put yourself in scenarios where you're exposed to new things. Visit a library or bookstore and explore an aisle you'd normally never walk down. Tinker. Try a new hobby. If you have always been an athlete, go to an art museum; if you're an artist, go to a sporting event. Bring words like *fun*, *play*, *explore*, *adventure*, and *spontaneity* back into your life. Follow people from different fields and backgrounds on social media. Shadow someone from a different department at work. Set up coffee with someone who inspires you.

This is how Satya Nadella, the celebrated CEO of Microsoft, found his talents. He struggled a lot when he was younger because he didn't know what he was good at. It wasn't school, where he got terrible grades. He loved cricket, but he wasn't good enough to make the playoff team. His dad kept trying to find new things for him to try out, and one day hit gold when he brought home the Sinclair ZX80, one of the first home computers. Nadella got sparked. This eventually led to a whole host of talents, including computer science and product development.

After doing these exercises, you'll end up with a list full of things that interest, excite, or inspire you—your potential, waiting to be unfolded.

STEP #2:
TURN YOUR POTENTIAL INTO A TALENT

Leonardo da Vinci was the son of a wealthy, well-respected man in Florence and grew up exposed to the city's renowned art and culture. He started drawing as a child, and his father arranged for him to apprentice with one of Florence's artists, the legendary Verrocchio. Leonardo ended up spending many years working in Verrocchio's studio, developing his artistic talent.

Charles Dickens had a rougher start. At the age of twelve, he had to go work at a boot-blacking factory to pay off his father's debts. After three years in the factory, Dickens was able to return to school. Eventually, he became a reporter, writing daily stories for newspapers and developing his writing talent.

Ada Lovelace was born to Lord Byron, the famous poet, and was encouraged by her mother to pursue her passionate interest in math and science. While working with her mentor, the celebrated mathematician Charles Babbage, Lovelace created the first computer program.

When you look at the life stories of many talented people, a pattern emerges: they are put into (or find their way into) environments that

To build your talent, practice it. Getting into flow will help it grow.

make it easier to turn their potential into a talent, where they can practice using it again and again and again.

That's not sufficient, though, according to the research of eminent psychologist Mihaly Csikszentmihalyi. Hard work is important, but what matters most is that you find a way to make that work enjoyable.

How can you make hard work fun? By getting into a "flow state." This is a different stage of consciousness in which you are totally absorbed in what you are doing and feeling one with the task at hand. It's an incredibly enjoyable experience that is intrinsically rewarding. It also fills you with motivation, inspiring you to go back for more, which, in turn, helps you get better and better at whatever you're doing.

In one study, Csikszentmihalyi analyzed a group of teenagers, trying to discern what differentiated those with talents. The talented teenagers found it enjoyable to build their talents, so they were more motivated and more determined to overcome challenges. He describes how Francis Crick, who helped discover the double-helix DNA structure, said that the single most important factor for his success was that he enjoyed his work. In Csikszentmihalyi's view, ideally "a person would be constantly growing while enjoying whatever he or she did." Flow helps you grow.

I learned about flow in graduate school, and although I understood it academically, I didn't truly get it until I met my partner, Alex, the most talented person I have ever met. When we first met, Alex had just become obsessed with relearning how to skateboard. I saw how hard he was working to master it, but I also saw just how much fun he was having. He quite simply glowed with joy.

Watching him, a lightbulb went off for me. I had always believed, deep down, that building a talent would be easy and fun. I was wrong. It is hard and fun.

It comes back to Old Happy outcomes and New Happy goals. There is a big difference between working hard to achieve an extrinsic goal and working hard to unfold who you really are. The former is draining; the latter is enlivening.

Everyone starts out as a beginner. But if you're put into an environment where you experience flow, again and again, you can quickly build a talent.

In a better world, every single person would grow up with an environment that does this. One study found that if you are born into a family in the top 1 percent of earners, you are ten times more likely to become an inventor. There are millions of "lost Einsteins"—women, members of marginalized communities, and people from lower-income families—who weren't given the support they needed to unlock their potential. It is an injustice to the many out there who don't get the support they deserve to grow into the people they really are, as well as a travesty for those of us who don't get to benefit from their gifts.

What we can do, however, is mimic this environment for ourselves. It starts with learning how to get into flow states. To do this, you need to match your skill with the challenge you're taking on. When you're just starting, the smallest task is enough of a challenge for your existing skills. As you get better, you can slowly increase the challenge level until you're taking on momentous projects (*Spirited Away*! The *Mona Lisa*!). Through repeated flow experiences, you can reach a level of mastery that was unimaginable at the beginning.

Choose an item from your potential list. Maybe you have identified that you are interested in teaching.

Think about a task in that area that you would feel comfortable doing right now. This will depend on how much experience you have, from never teaching anything to having years of experience in a classroom.

Amp up the challenge of that task about 10 percent above your comfort level. If the challenge is too high, it becomes stressful, which makes you want to quit. If the challenge is too low, though, it becomes boring, which also makes you want to quit. If you have never taught before, a good challenge might be, "Teach my friend how to write a cover letter." If you have more experience, a good challenge could be, "Spend an hour drafting a brand-new curriculum outline."

Then do it.

You can repeat this process again and again, each time amping up the challenge to meet your new skill level.

Flow is so powerful because it helps you tap into a different state of consciousness in which you can focus for hours. Anthropologist David Graeber and archaeologist David Wengrow point out that in our normal state, we can focus on a thought or an idea for about seven seconds. It's very hard to unfold your potential in seven-second increments.

There's also a second state of consciousness that can last for hours, Graeber and Wengrow point out: connecting with other people. We can spend hours engaged in conversation, play, or practice alongside others. This is another tool we can use to turn our potential into a talent.

Famously, Serena Williams grew up playing tennis with her older sister, Venus, a fellow superstar. As Serena described their dynamic in an interview, "We bring out the best in each other. I know when I play her, I have to play some of my best tennis. She does, too . . . throughout our career, we have pushed each other to be the best that we can be."

Hayao Miyazaki's mentor was his first supervisor, a man named Yasuo Ōtsuka, who continually championed his work, promoting him into important roles and bringing him onto new projects. "Whenever I reached a turning point, Ōtsuka would always appear and invite me to move in a new direction," Miyazaki said. "He's the person who helped me most."

Consider how you can build your own community—of peers, those who are more experienced, and masters.

- Peers: Many educational programs use this approach, like master of fine arts degrees, in which students are put into writing groups for critique and discussion. Create your own group of people who are working toward similar talents, and meet on a regular basis to support and coach each other.

- Experienced: Approach someone who might be able to mentor you. Meeting once a month or a few times a year with another person can have a profound impact on your growth. (Those of you who are more experienced, this is an incredible way to use your gifts to help, too!)
- Masters: You might not be able to connect with them directly, but you can read their biographies, watch documentaries, engage with their work, and study their influences.

Helping each other turn potential into talent is another wonderful path to happiness.

STEP #3:
KEEP EVOLVING YOUR TALENT

Your true self doesn't want to stay in one place. It wants to keep expanding. It *needs* to keep expanding.

As you become more skilled at using your talent, you will need to continually increase the level of challenge to keep experiencing flow states. This is why a focus on New Happy authentic actions over outcomes is so important: there is no destination to reach. As long as you are alive, you will be in the process of becoming yourself.

The writer Zadie Smith once shared a piece of advice that she found in choreographer Martha Graham's biography. Graham describes how important it is to stay connected to your inner potential, no matter what that looks like, writing, "There is a vitality, a life force, an energy, a quickening that is translated through you into action, and because there is only one of you in all of time, this expression is unique."

Graham points out that one of our biggest obstacles to fulfilling our potential is, in fact, ourselves. She urges us to be careful not to block that life force in any way, because if we do, it will be lost forever—the unique talent that can only be expressed through you. It is

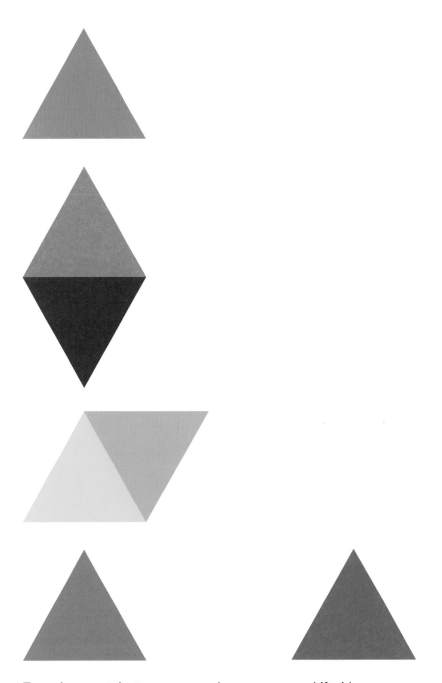

To evolve your talent, you can go deeper, you can shift sideways, or you can leap into something entirely new.

not yours to decide whether or not your talent is good or important or useful; it is your responsibility to simply keep your channel open so that you can express it.

You are not your talent. You are the one expressing your talent. And sometimes that expression might change. If you have a talent that has left you feeling bored or uninspired, that's a sign to go deeper, move sideways, or take a leap.

Go Deeper

Charles Dickens didn't just write novels; he tried his hand at magazine articles, short stories, and plays, too.

You can go deeper with your talent by looking for an environment that will challenge you (like finding a new job, joining a community of people, or taking a class) or by setting yourself a task that's much more ambitious than anything you have taken on before (a writer taking on their first book, a builder taking on a more complex project).

Move Sideways

After Julia Child wrote her seminal cookbook, she starred in television shows, helped found the American Institute of Wine and Food, and worked in childhood food education.

Expand your perspective, and think about your talent as a part of a broader constellation. For example:

- A talent for art is a part of a broader constellation of "creation talents," like filmmaking, design, photography, or fashion.
- A talent for customer service is a part of a broader constellation of "connection talents," like volunteering, organizing, leading, sales, or public speaking.
- A talent for event planning is a part of a broader constellation of "organizational talents," like leadership, business administration, operations, or coordination.

Make a Leap

Aside from art, da Vinci spent many years studying the human body, mastering mathematics, and designing flying machines, robots, and weapons (well before we had the technology to build them). What connected these pursuits? He wanted to push beyond all existing knowledge and wasn't content to do that in just one field.

You can look at your own talents and ask yourself, "What's the deeper motivation that's driving my talent? Where else could I direct it?"

As you express your talents, that action ends up benefitting the world—not just in what you do with it, but by how it changes you as a person. Csikszentmihalyi argues that the person who constantly pursues flow can become their most evolved self: it doesn't just help you to personally grow, but also increases your ability to contribute. This is what "being your best self" really means.

KEEP YOUR TALENT A GIFT

Talents are the gifts that are most easily warped by Old Happy, the way a piece of wood gets warped in the rain.

Many of us use our talents in our jobs, and sometimes it can seem like our talent defines who we are. The Old Happy forces of individualism, capitalism, and domination encourage this: they want to put you in a box, and they want you to stay there. "You're just an electrician," or "You're just an accountant," or "You're just a nurse." You can't be limited like this. There is so much potential within you, always able to be expressed in new ways.

You do not have to use your talent to make money. You can use it anywhere:

- If you have a talent for motivating people, you could use it to keep your friends hopeful in hard times.
- If you have a talent for creating, you could use it to start a knitting hobby.

- If you have a talent for entertaining, you could use it to throw delightful dinner parties for your friends and family.

If your environment for your talent changes, such as when you're laid off, you're navigating an illness, or your life responsibilities are shifting, or if you decide you want to develop an entirely new talent altogether, your inner potential will find a new expression. If you have ever had a talent, that means you know how to build another one. This is a meta-talent, or a talent for building talents. All you need to do is to get back on the invisible path.

Because some talents are prioritized and rewarded by society, they can come to seem more important than others. Not true. Every talent serves an important purpose. Remember your place in the chain. All gifts matter; all gifts connect; all gifts add up. External rewards can even make you forget why you started using your talent in the first place: to unfold your inner powers and make a difference, not to gain fame or acclaim from others. Don't let Old Happy turn your authentic action into an outcome.

Your talent doesn't have to reach hundreds or thousands or millions of people to be meaningful. In fact, it's the moments of individual connection that usually have the greatest impact on your fulfillment and sense of purpose. Yes, Julia Child's recipes are renowned for their elegance. But are they as meaningful as the first meal your child, a budding chef, makes for you?

It's not how many you reach. It's that you reach. That you, a human being, are there to use your talent to help another human being when they need it. To quote Viktor Frankl, "Whether a life is fulfilled does not depend on how great one's radius of action is, but rather only on whether the circle is fully filled out."

KEY TAKEAWAYS

- There are three steps to building a talent: uncover your potential, turn it into a talent, and keep evolving it.

- Uncover your potential by looking for a spark: moments of interest, curiosity, and excitement.

- Turn your potential into a talent through 1) facilitating flow states and 2) working collaboratively or in a group.

- Over time, your talent will evolve. You can go deeper into what you're already doing, move sideways into a related field, or take a leap into a new domain.

13

Wisdom:
You Know More Than
You Realize

One Saturday afternoon in 2016, as I wandered through the San Francisco Museum of Modern Art, I was captivated by an exhibit from the artist Susan O'Malley. On brightly colored canvases, short sentences were printed in bold capital letters, profoundly joyful in their simplicity:

LISTEN TO YOUR HEART

EVERYTHING WILL BE OKAY

IT IS POSSIBLE

IT'S NOT A DUMB IDEA

YOU ALREADY KNOW WHAT YOU NEED

The exhibit was titled *Advice from My 80-Year-Old Self.* O'Malley had asked one hundred people, of every age and all walks of life, what advice their older self would give them in that exact moment. She called them community pep talks.

Their answers show us something so important about wisdom: we all have it. O'Malley knew that we just need the right prompt to help us to tap into it.

Have you ever had someone ask you a good question and then been surprised by the words that came out of your mouth? You started sharing things that were authentic and true but that you had never expressed before. A good prompt shows you the wisdom that is alive within you.

There is no single definition of wisdom within the research, but most scientists agree that it involves using your life experiences to grow as a person, becoming someone who can contribute to the well-being of others through guidance, problem-solving, and navigating uncertainty. As the sociologist Monika Ardelt points out, "Wisdom needs to be realized through reflection on personal experiences."

Building on this research, I define "wisdom gifts" as insights or understandings that come from your personal experience. When you act upon that wisdom, through the way you live, an action you take, something you make, or the way you support others, it turns into a gift.

Gifts of wisdom are used to catalyze movements, inspire initiatives, start programs and services, make good decisions, and solve important problems. They can range from momentous insights about the nature of the world to strategies that solve specific problems.

A lot of people don't believe that they have any wisdom. This is ridiculous. *Of course* you have wisdom. You are the only person who has ever lived your life and the only person who *will* ever live your life! There are treasures within you that could ease broken hearts and solve problems and transform lives. You just haven't been given the right prompt to unlock it.

THE POWER OF A PERSPECTIVE SHIFT

In 1990, psychology PhD student Elizabeth Newton ran a fascinating experiment. She gathered one hundred fifty people and divided them into two groups. The first group was the "tappers," and the second group was the "listeners." The tappers were told to think about a song and then tap out the melody on the table. Afterward, they were asked

Look at your life so far. Shift your perspective and see:
you have so much wisdom that could help others.

to guess how likely it would be for the listener to guess the song. The tappers guessed that about half of the listeners would know what the tune was. In reality, only two out of one hundred fifty people guessed correctly—about 0.01 percent.

This finding was so striking that it got its own name: the curse of knowledge. Once we know something, it's hard to imagine what it's like not to know it. We hear the song in our heads, so we assume everyone else can hear it, too. Instead of thinking about what the other person needs to hear to succeed at the task of identifying the tune, we are thinking about what we, ourselves, are hearing.

This is exactly what prevents us from discovering our own wisdom. We are thinking about *ourselves* instead of considering what others need. We have to decenter ourselves and ask, "What do I know that could be useful to someone else?"

Multiple studies have shown how effective this shift can be. In one, researchers asked participants to first think about one of their own personal challenges and then imagine it was a friend's challenge and they had to give them advice. Imagining advising a friend led to wiser answers. In another study, Americans were asked to think about polarizing American political issues from the perspective of either an American living in the United States or an Icelandic person living in Iceland. Those imagining themselves as Icelandic were able to analyze their own American issues in a wiser manner.

In the following sections, we'll look at four key sources of wisdom in our lives, and the four prompts that help you unlock them:

- Your life journey: "What have I learned in my life that could benefit others?"
- Your accomplishments: "What have I achieved and how would I guide someone else to do the same?"
- Your difficulties: "What pain have I experienced that I can prevent for others?"
- Your connections: "What can I learn from other people?"

YOUR LIFE JOURNEY

My mom began swimming as a preteen, eventually getting serious about it as a teenager. After spending her high school years training, she became an All-American athlete at the University of Michigan and eventually competed at the 1984 Olympics. In 1985, she retired— and never swam again.

After her retirement, she struggled to find her place in the world, searching for something that would build upon her life experiences and bring her a similar sense of fulfillment. This search lasted twenty-seven years. She tried many things, devoting herself to them with her full, athlete intensity: running a franchise, volunteering in the community, and caring for our family. All the while, she felt like she was missing something.

In 2013, a fellow Olympian, tragically died by suicide. My mom had no idea how much they were suffering. Their death made her realize that she wasn't alone in struggling after leaving sports. There were so many other athletes out there, feeling lost and unsure of how to navigate their new, post-sport life.

This galvanized her to use her life experience to help other athletes. She spent the next five years conducting research, mapping out both the promises and pitfalls of leaving sport, and then turned it into a book. Now, she spends her days supporting Olympians around the world, preparing them for life after sports so that they have the tools and support they need to navigate the transition.

Everyone has a unique life journey, and with that comes unique wisdom. Discover yours by using the first wisdom prompt: "What have I learned in my life that could benefit others?" Here are a few examples:

- "I was the first Black woman to become partner at my firm. I now mentor underrepresented women in the field and help companies become more equitable."
- "When I immigrated to the United States, I had no idea how to build financial credit. I had to figure it out all by myself. I

now work with my church's refugee services to give new immigrants a simple and easy guide."

- "Growing up, my sister had a disability and I witnessed her unable to participate in a lot of typical childhood events. I use that experience to design more inclusive play spaces."

Looking back on our lives from a distance, we can identify patterns and lessons, as the famous quote from Søren Kierkegaard reminds us: "Life must be understood backward. But then one forgets the other principle, that it must be lived forward."

YOUR ACCOMPLISHMENTS

One of the greatest things about our world is that there is always someone who wants to do what you have done, and there is always someone who has done what you want to do.

Some people are in a different stage or season of life that you have already experienced (going to school, getting a job, having kids). Others are pursuing goals that you have already achieved (start a business, hike a mountain, learn a specific skill).

This wisdom—the wisdom of accomplishments—is one of the ways that we can help each other. We pass down wisdom through a web of relationships, following other people's tracks and guiding others in our footsteps, each time making the path uniquely our own.

Consider your milestones that stand out as moments of growth, achievement, and transition. The second wisdom prompt is: "What have I accomplished, and how would I guide someone else to do the same?"

In my research, I came across a wonderful story that serves as an example of this type of wisdom—as well as the way that wisdom can end up changing lives.

In 2006, Erin Lockwood was a teacher at Xavier High School in New York City. She asked her students to write letters to famous authors, asking for them to come visit and teach their creative process.

Kurt Vonnegut, the author of *Slaughterhouse-Five*, was the only one who answered. In his letter, he provided the students with an assignment, carefully specifying that they were not to share it within anyone — not even their teacher, Ms. Lockwood. Write a six-line poem, he told them. It can be about anything, but it must be rhymed. He told them that they must try as hard as they possibly can, giving that poem everything that they had until they felt it was the best that it could be.

Then, he told them, tear it up. Rip it apart into tiny pieces and throw them out into different garbage cans.

The finished end result of the poem is not what matters. What matters is how writing that poem will change you as a person. You will find, he says, that you have "made your soul grow."

Through his achievements as an author, Vonnegut had discovered a secret of creativity. Making art makes your soul grow; if you want to be creative, focus on that. He passed on this wisdom with his letter.

I was able to track down Lockwood and asked her about the assignment. "As soon as they finished the letters, I sent them off," she told me, laughing, "never expecting to hear anything again." Then one day, someone left a note on her desk: Kurt Vonnegut called. She thought it was a joke at first.

When they connected on the phone, Vonnegut told Lockwood how touched he was to receive the letters. In a lovely turn of events, Lockwood told him that his book *Breakfast of Champions* was her favorite book in high school and influenced her choice to become an English teacher. They hung up, and she thought that was the end of it. But then his letter arrived, addressed to the class.

Lockwood put me in touch with one of the students who wrote the original letters to Vonnegut, Michael Perrin, who is now himself a teacher in New York City.

Perrin told me that what inspired him the most was that although Vonnegut acknowledged that he couldn't come to visit, he was willing to do what he could instead, passing on "incredibly powerful and downright radical words of encouragement for teenagers at that time." Perrin described this as a profound example of sharing wisdom whenever you can.

Both Lockwood and Perrin told me of how much they have thought back to the wisdom in Vonnegut's letter. Lockwood, who left teaching to become a therapist, referenced how his words influenced her. Perrin shared that he often reminds himself of Vonnegut's words, using it to guide his teaching.

Vonnegut could so easily have ignored the students' letters, but instead, he took the time to craft a wise response, one that has had ripple effects in their lives twenty years later. He passed away just a few months after sending the letter.

YOUR CHALLENGES

The psychiatrist Elisabeth Kübler-Ross, originator of the Five Stages of Grief, wrote in her book, *Death: The Final Stage of Growth*:

> The most beautiful people we have known are those who have known defeat, known suffering, known struggle, known loss, and have found their way out of the depths. These persons have an appreciation, a sensitivity, and an understanding of life that fills them with compassion, gentleness, and a deep loving concern. Beautiful people do not just happen.

Wise people choose to see pain and struggles in a different way: not just as an experience they personally need to get through, but something that can be transformed to help another person. They know that there are others out there who are suffering and who could benefit from their knowledge. As it turns out, this choice can also help you to more effectively cope in hard times, connecting you with a greater purpose and strengthening your resilience.

To discover the wisdom from your challenges, prompt yourself: "What pain have I experienced that I could prevent for others?"

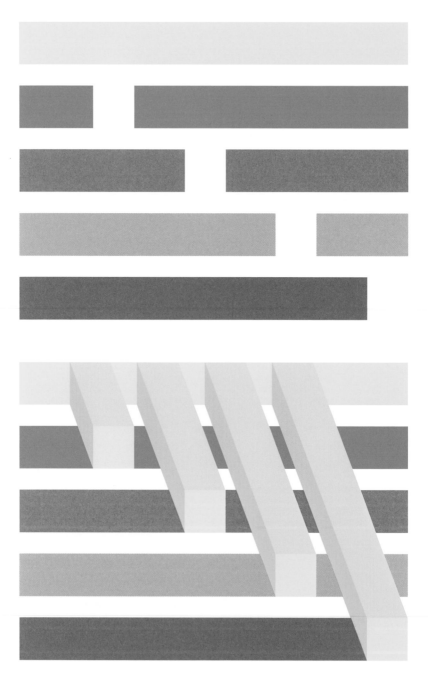

The wisdom from your past experiences can help people
who are struggling in the present moment.

I recently read a story about a librarian named Barbara Weedman. Years ago, Weedman was a single mother who knew how difficult it was to navigate a world with so few child- and family-friendly spaces.

When her library underwent a renovation, she proposed building something that would help single parents: specific workstations that had an attached carrel for babies. The parent could use the computer while their baby lay next to them, surrounded by decorated wooden panels with quotes from books. In this way, Weedman was able to turn her pain into something that helped others. The article went viral, with many other libraries reaching out to learn how they could make similar workstations.

Another example comes from Oprah Winfrey, who grew up in extreme poverty and experienced sexual abuse as a child in rural Mississippi. Throughout these difficulties, she held on to her dreams of becoming a journalist and making a difference in the world. In sharing her own path of transformation, Winfrey empowered others to follow in her footsteps. Sometimes, all it takes to pass on your wisdom is the courageous choice to talk about the challenges that you have been through.

WHAT YOU CAN LEARN FROM OTHERS

Rabbi Simcha Bunim, a Polish religious leader in the 1800s, taught that you should keep two pieces of paper in your pocket at all times. On the first, write, "I am a speck of dust." On the other, write, "The world was created for me."

This is how we want to treat our wisdom: "I have important insights, perspectives, and experiences to share with the world," and "There is so much that I do not know." You know more than you realize and less than you think.

Scientists agree that an essential part of wisdom is possessing intellectual humility. A wise person is willing to admit not only when they don't know something, but also when they are wrong. They recognize that any wisdom has a limit and a specific context and that it isn't necessarily universal. And most importantly, they know that when you become too assured of your wisdom, you become an unwise person.

To tap into this wisdom, prompt yourself: "What can others teach me?"

Not a single one of us knows everything. It's yet another reason why we need each other. We serve as one another's teachers, guides, and helpers.

Sometimes this wisdom is explicitly given. In the 1930s, the activist and writer Pauli Murray met Eleanor Roosevelt, then the First Lady. A few years later, Murray wrote Roosevelt a letter to protest Southern segregation. When Roosevelt responded, an unlikely friendship bloomed between the two. Murray challenged Roosevelt to see the world in a completely different way, shaping her actions in years to come and affecting legislation, administrative priorities, and human rights initiatives.

Other times, this wisdom passed on through observation. True wisdom is embodied, meaning that you can learn a great deal from watching the way that someone else communicates and behaves. For example, my partner Alex's mom has been a nurse for more than twenty years. When Alex was sick, she was far away in Australia, yet she still became a lifeline for me—not only for her medical knowledge, but also for her embodied understanding of caring for people who are sick and scared and sad. I often tried to emulate her in hard moments, asking myself, "How would Shelagh respond to this challenge?"

You can draw upon and learn from anyone's wisdom using this powerful strategy. Think of someone—whether you know them personally or not—who possesses wisdom that you do not presently have. Imagine what they would do if they were in your shoes. When you take action in accordance with their wisdom, you start to build it within you.

YOUR WISDOM NEEDS TO
BE PASSED ON

In a fascinating paper, biological anthropologist Joseph Henrich and psychologist Michael Muthukrishna ask: Why are we humans smarter than other animals, and how have we managed to survive challenging circumstances, build new innovations, and find ways to thrive?

The instinctive answer for most people, they point out, is the individualistic one: there are a few great people, and they make huge strides that the rest of us benefit from. Their paper argues that the opposite is true. Our progress is not based on great people; it's based on the greatness of people as a whole. We have built what they call a "collective brain," or the knowledge and wisdom we have accumulated over thousands of years. This collective brain is what helps us navigate our current challenges and progress forward toward a better future.

There are so many different ways to turn your wisdom into a gift, and contribute to our collective brain, such as:

- Creating programs or services
- Communicating in writing or verbally
- Implementing new systems
- Teaching
- Offering another perspective
- Speaking up
- Making something
- Telling your story
- Being yourself

Imagine how much more powerful our collective brain would become if all of us shared our wisdom. Take what you have learned, and pass it on.

We have a responsibility to pass our wisdom on to other people.
That is how we reach new heights and build a better world.

BRING TOGETHER ALL OF
YOUR GIFTS

You have now learned about your three types of gifts: humanity, talent, and wisdom. You possess extraordinary goodness within you in the form of love, potential, and perspective; by cultivating and expressing these, you can experience profound happiness.

When I was writing this chapter, I wanted to reach out to Susan O'Malley, the artist from that exhibit all those years ago, to see if I could talk to her about her work and express my gratitude to her.

In trying to find her, I found out something tragic. After years of trying to get pregnant, she and her husband had conceived twin girls. Three days before her scheduled C-section, O'Malley collapsed. Unbeknownst to anyone, she had a tumor attached to her heart. The doctors weren't able to save her or her children. I was in tears reading about this loss: so wrong, so devastating, and so, so unfair.

As I read the tributes to her life, I learned about how O'Malley had a dream for a world that was filled with more love, connection, and joy. She made it her life's mission to build that, one piece of art and one question at a time.

After she died, her friends chose one of her pieces, printed thousands of copies of it, and placed it all over the Bay Area to help her achieve her vision. They chose a piece from the exhibit I had visited, a beautiful rainbow gradient that read:

**IT WILL BE MORE BEAUTIFUL THAN YOU
COULD EVER IMAGINE**

The story I wanted to tell O'Malley was about that piece. There was one day when I was driving home from work, in a state of complete despair over Alex's illness. I felt completely hopeless. And then, stopped in traffic, I saw her print painted on the side of a building in gigantic letters. It was a beacon of hope.

It wasn't only her wisdom that affected me, though. It was all of her gifts, brought together in that piece of work. There was her wisdom of knowing that people have the answers inside of them and that those answers can help others. There was her talent, of conveying those words in an arresting and beautiful piece of artwork. And there was her humanity, her deep desire to bring more love to the world.

In bringing together all of her gifts, she was able to reach through space and time to touch me in the exact moment that I needed it—doing what only she could, a contribution that could never be replicated or copied, for it was born from her true self. I wish I could have told her how much that moment meant to me. Thank you, Susan. You lifted me up at the exact moment I needed it most.

You, using your gifts, will lift people up, too. You, using your gifts, will do something only you can do. You, using your gifts, will help people you know and people you don't in ways that they'll remember for the rest of their lives.

KEY TAKEAWAYS

- Wisdom comes from your life experiences.

- We struggle to see our own wisdom. In order to unlock it, focus on how your experiences can help other people.

- There are four key places to start looking for your wisdom: your life journey, your achievements, your difficulties, and your connections.

- When you pass your wisdom on to others, you aren't only helping one person—you are also contributing to our collective brain, which enables positive progress for society.

PART FIVE

Serve the World

14

The Need That Binds
Us All Together

When you think of Albert Einstein, a few things probably come to mind: iconic genius, $E = mc^2$, great hair.

But here's something you don't know about the most famous scientist of all time: he was passionate about living a New Happy life. Of course, he didn't use those exact words, but he makes it clear in his writings and behaviors.

In a commencement speech given at Swarthmore College in 1938, Einstein described New Happy, saying:

> Every individual should have the opportunity to develop the gifts which may be latent in him. Alone in that way can the individual obtain the satisfaction to which he is justly entitled; and alone in that way can the community achieve its richest flourishing.

Einstein calls this experience of using your gifts "a satisfaction," but I think that's wildly underselling it.

When you use your gifts, what you feel is so much more than any single word can encompass. It's a profound form of happiness: a sense of purpose coupled with feelings of daily joy; endless motivation coexisting with contentment; resilience that supports you during setbacks;

determination that imbues you with courage; an experience that brings you closer to yourself, to others, and to the world all at the same time.

What about the second part Einstein mentions, that this helps the world "achieve its richest flourishing"?

This is the question we'll be answering in this chapter. It's the last piece of the New Happy puzzle, the final step we need to take before we can use our gifts and experience the profound happiness they bring us.

We need to realize that not only are we connected to the whole world, but we are completely dependent upon it for our happiness.

WE ARE ALL CONNECTED

On January 31, 1971, Edgar Mitchell left Earth for the moon. On February 5, the *Apollo 14* mission landed in the moon's Fra Mauro Formation, where he and Alan Shepard spent thirty-three hours gathering rock and soil samples as well as setting up experiments to send data back to Earth.

Mitchell was never the same again. As he described it, it was the instant dawning of a new sort of consciousness—one that wasn't limited to his separate self, but encompassing of all other beings who shared the planet with him. He felt an immediate sense of anger about the inequalities and injustices of the world, alongside an intense desire to do something to help fix them.

Scientists call this "the overview effect." When astronauts go to space, they experience a sense of awe that blows their worldview to smithereens, leading to a new awareness of our interdependence.

You don't have to go to space to realize this. This is the exact journey we have been going on throughout this book. With every chapter, you have been changing the way you see yourself: from separate to connected; then expanding to connect with more and more people through giving and receiving; and now, connecting with the whole world.

This greatest form of connection has long been practiced by Indigenous peoples and cultures, and shamefully destroyed or suppressed by colonizers. According to Tink Tinker, a scholar of Native Ameri-

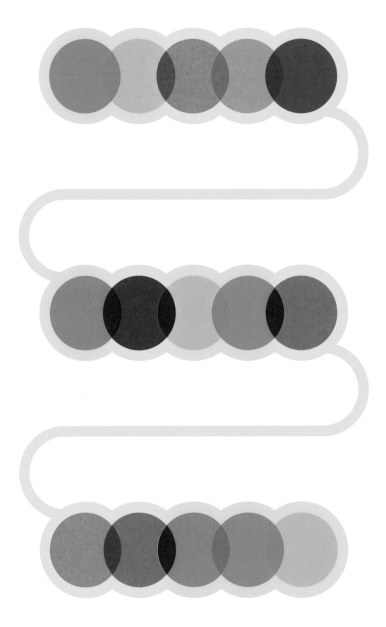

You are not only connected to the people around you, but
profoundly interconnected with everyone on the planet.

can history, the key difference comes back to our worldviews. For example, Indigenous Hawaiian worldviews see everything as connected, believing "personal balance can only be constituted in the relational context of the community whole." In the Bantu philosophy of *ubuntu*, the core abiding value is seeing yourself as inextricably connected to others. Research has linked these worldviews to mental, physical, community, and ecological health benefits.

It is this connection to the world that motivates and inspires us to contribute to it.

When someone buys a car for themselves, they say, "It's my car." When a couple buys a car together, they say, "It's our car."

When an employee finishes a solo project, they say, "It's my work." When a team works on a project together, they say, "It's our work."

When humans are separate from one another, they say, "That's not my problem." But when they are connected to one another, they say, "How can I help you?"

HOW TO IDENTIFY WITH THE WORLD

One day in Poland during the summer of 1942, a woman named Balwina answered her door and discovered a young boy: dirty, hungry, terrified, numb with grief, and all alone. She recognized him as the son of a man she had traded with before the Nazis invaded. The boy's name was Samuel Oliner, and he had miraculously escaped from the Bobowa ghetto moments before the Nazis had murdered all of the occupants, including his whole family.

Immediately, she brought him inside, even though the penalty for sheltering Jewish people was death. Balwina listened to him, fed him, and devised a plan to help him survive. She gave Samuel a fake Polish name and helped him find a job on a distant farm where no neighbors would recognize him. She even sent her son over to visit, pretending they were old school friends, making Samuel's story more plausible.

Thanks to Balwina's courage, he survived the war. After emigrating to the United States, Samuel devoted his life to the study of altruism: why people like Balwina help others. He teamed up with his wife, Pearl Oliner, a fellow sociologist, to study those people who saved Jewish people during World War II.

The Oliners' essential insight was that when you see others as a part of you, you want to help them. Balwina didn't see Samuel as an "other," or someone who was different from her. She saw him as a fellow human being.

Research by the political scientist Kristen Monroe confirms the Oliners' work. She interviewed heroes who risked their lives to save people, rushing into burning buildings or jumping onto subway tracks. They all had one thing in common: they saw themselves as connected to everyone, a part of a greater humanity.

If we don't connect with all of humanity, we run the risk of only connecting with some people—those who are most like us. We have a tendency to categorize people into groups ("New Yorkers" or "Christians" or "Americans") and then prioritize the people in our own group. Depending on who we are deeming as "the other," this in-group can change, as described in the famous Bedouin proverb: "Me against my brother, my brother and I against my cousin, and all of us against the stranger." These divisions can lead to oppression, violence, genocide, and war.

Contrary to popular belief, we are not doomed to divide ourselves in these ways. Extensive research shows that although we do categorize ourselves, these categories are very flexible. Multiple experiments demonstrate that we divide the world into groups at the toss of a coin.

There's a clever study that proves how flexible these labels are, a twist on the Good Samaritan study we discussed in chapter 11.

Researchers recruited a group of Manchester United soccer fans and asked them to focus on their identity as a fan: how much it meant to them, how much happiness it gave them, and how connected they felt to fellow Manchester United fans. They were then told to walk to another building to watch a video. As they did, an accident was staged in front of them. A researcher tripped, crying in pain. Here was the twist: he was wearing either a Manchester United shirt, a plain shirt, or a shirt of their hated long-time rivals, Liverpool. Would they help this "other"?

Ninety-two percent of participants helped the person in the Manchester United shirt, the person in their in-group. Only 30 percent helped the person in the Liverpool shirt, and 33 percent of them helped the person wearing a plain shirt. Help was given to the person who was the most like them.

The researchers expected this. What they really wanted to know was if they could change the way the participants related to people who weren't like them.

They ran the experiment again with new people. This time, though, participants were asked to reflect on a higher-level version of their identity: soccer fans. This would encompass Manchester United fans but also fans of Everton, Arsenal, and Chelsea—and even their Liverpudlian rivals. This time, when the person fell in front of them, the participants were equally likely to help the Liverpool fans as they were the Manchester United fans. And they were significantly less likely to help the plain-shirted person.

I wonder what would have happened if the researchers had abstracted their identities even further, asking them to focus on the fact that they were all human beings. Would more of them have helped the plain-shirted person? I suspect so.

This is something we all can practice. Think about the part of your identity that you identify with the most. Then, abstract it out, further and further, trying to encompass broader groups at each stage. It might look like this:

- I'm a Texan.
- I'm an American.
- I'm a North American.
- I'm a human.
- I'm a living being.

Or:

- I'm a designer.
- I'm a creative person.
- I'm a person.
- I'm a living being.

At a physical level, you *are* connected to everyone. Some scientists posit that every single human alive today shares one common ancestor, born between 1400 BCE and 55 CE. We are all related. Maybe it's no wonder scientists like Einstein advocate for this orientation to the world: it's the logical thing to do.

YOU NEED THE WORLD

At close to midnight on September 10, 2010, Steve Jobs sent himself an email. It had been a little over a week since he had been on stage in California, announcing the latest iPhone software release as well as a slew of other updates to their products like Apple TV and the iPod.

In this email, he writes, not about the success of his business and the acclaim for his products, but of his dependence on other people. He reflects on how every part of his life relies upon people: the food he eats, the clothing he wears, the language he speaks, the mathematics he uses, the freedom that others fought for, the medical care he receives, and the technology he uses every day. He ends it by describing his complete and total love for his fellow human beings, recognizing that he would not survive or be able to find any happiness without them.

We are the constant beneficiaries of other people's gifts in action. Billions of people whom we will never know have contributed to our happiness. This is what Aristotle called the common good, the collective well-being that makes it possible to experience our own individual well-being.

Even the simplest daily tasks showcase your dependence on the world. A few years ago, the artist Thomas Thwaites set out to try to

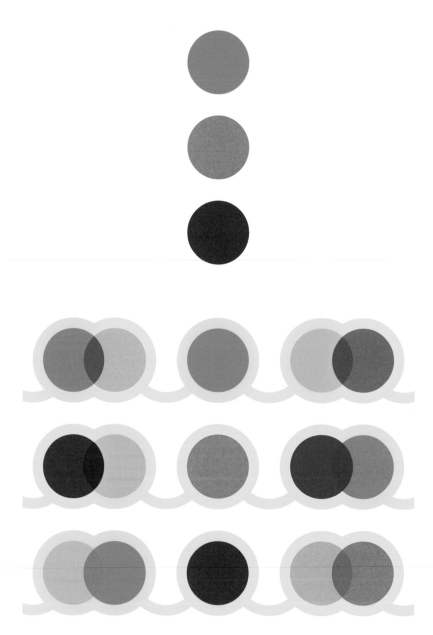

There is not a single person who stands alone. You are dependent
upon countless others and constantly benefit from their gifts.

rebuild a toaster from scratch by himself. He purchased the cheapest toaster he could, which cost less than five dollars. When he took it apart, he discovered that it was made of 404 unique parts, the result of a complex chain of human development that all had to come together for someone to crisp a piece of bread.

Einstein, too, embraced this truth. He wrote, "A hundred times a day, I remind myself that my inner and outer lives are based on the labors of other people, living and dead . . . and that I must exert myself in order to give in the same measure that I have received."

Jobs and Einstein are held up as two of the greatest "world-changers" we have ever had. No one would deny their impact. At the same time, they didn't do any of it alone. They were the first to admit that.

For example, as a student, Einstein often skipped his physics classes, finding them boring; he used his friend Marcel Grossmann's notes to study for his tests. Grossmann later partnered with him to help him develop and evolve his theories when Einstein begged him, "You must help me, or else I'll go crazy." It was Grossmann's father who got Einstein a job at the Swiss Patent Office. There he was tasked with reviewing all new inventions, which helped him advance his own work. When Einstein was stuck on a problem, he would talk to his friend Michele Besso, whom he called "the best sounding board in Europe." When he needed to escape the Nazis, he was provided with protection by the Belgian royal family, given a hideaway in England, and then welcomed by the United States.

Fanning out alongside every figure whom history calls "great" are a field of people who helped them—most of whom go unrecognized, but all of whom contributed their own gifts to a greater good.

We all have greatness within us, but individual greatness is only unlocked by being a part of a collective.

THE WORLD NEEDS YOU

In 2008, the astronaut Ron Garan went on a mission to the International Space Station, where, similar to Edgar Mitchell, he, too, experienced the overview effect. In his book *The Orbital Perspective*, he described how worldview transformation was followed by a deep sense of sadness:

> I couldn't help thinking of the nearly one billion people who don't have clean water to drink, the countless number who go to bed hungry every night, the social injustice, conflicts, and poverty that remain pervasive across the planet . . . We are all traveling together on the planet and if we all looked at the world from that perspective, we would see that nothing is impossible.

Our world has no shortage of problems. When we're disconnected from our common humanity, it's easy to look at them and say, "That doesn't affect me right now, so I don't have to worry about it."

Even if the problem does affect you, it might feel far too big and complex to be something you can do anything about. You're only one person, after all. Someone else will come along and fix it.

No one else is coming to save us. We are the only ones who can do it. The world needs us.

It was Viktor Frankl, Holocaust survivor and author of *Man's Search for Meaning*, who counseled to stop asking what we want from life and start asking what life wants from us. Just as a baby cries when she needs food, our world's problems are the cries that it needs *us*. All around us, people are suffering, yet we have been ignoring their cries, leading to a steady degradation of the common good through evermore, ever-expanding problems.

If, for example, in thirty years, we have failed to halt global warming's progression, will we be worrying about productivity and career growth and the many other topics that concern us today? Of course not. We will be too busy trying to survive in 110°F heat and watching in horror as entire populations are killed, all the while wishing we had done something differently when we still had the chance.

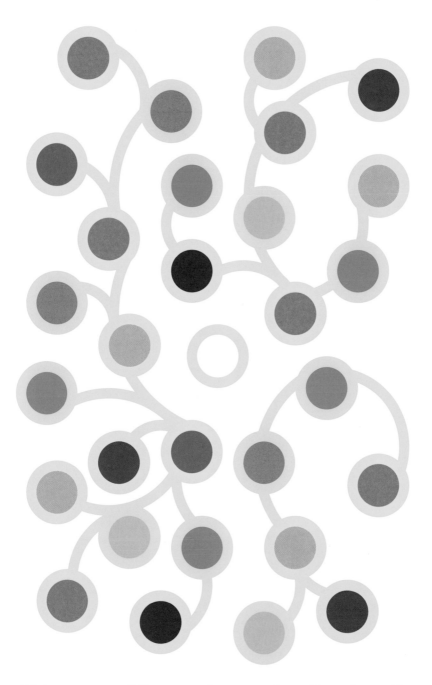

We have a responsibility to contribute our unique gifts to the world.
That creates happiness for you and a happier world for all of us.

In fact, Aristotle argued that personal happiness is impossible unless you're contributing to the common good. The word *idiot* derives from the Greek word *idiota*. It was used, in his time, to describe those people who refused to contribute to the common good.

All of the world's problems could be solved by using our gifts. You can use what makes you different to contribute to what we share—now knowing that this is what fulfills your needs, too. In answering the world's cries, you will find the life purpose that you long for. This is why Einstein said we should see the world's problems as "opportunities for joyous service towards a better life."

All of our greatest heroes used their gifts to address a need in the world:

- Jonas Salk, eradicating polio
- Nelson Mandela, ending apartheid
- Ai Weiwei, advocating for human rights
- Malala Yousafzai, ensuring girls can access education

What will it be for you? What problem will you help to solve? What need will you meet with your gifts?

In the 1990s, the renowned science-fiction author Octavia Butler was at a book signing for her Parable series, which is set in 2027, describing a world devastated by climate change. A student came up to her and asked, "Do you believe that the future you wrote about is going to happen?" Butler pointed out that she didn't make up the problems—she simply imagined how they would continue to evolve in the future if we didn't act. The student asked her how we could fix it. She replied: "There's no magic bullet. Instead there are thousands of answers—at least. You can be one of them if you choose to be."

This mutual need binds us together. The only way you can survive in the world is to receive help from others, and the only way you can thrive in this world is to offer help to others.

THE GREATEST GOAL IN THE WORLD

One summer in the 1950s, twenty-two boys were brought to a summer camp and observed for three weeks, unaware that their actions were being documented by their camp counselors, who were actually social science researchers.

The boys were divided into two groups. The groups arrived on separate buses, believing they were alone. Each group bonded, naming themselves the Rattlers and the Eagles, designing T-shirts, and making flags.

After a week, the researchers shocked the boys by introducing the two groups. It was an instant rivalry that the researchers intensified through a Rattlers versus Eagles competition, leading to name-calling and flag-burning.

Then the real purpose of the experiment arrived: could the researchers bring the groups together? First, they got them to spend time together, which did not work; a shared meal turned into a food fight.

Then they gave them a problem that couldn't be solved by one group alone. The researchers shut off the camp's drinking water, claiming "vandals" had tampered with it. The Rattlers and Eagles investigated separately, agreed that it was an obstructed faucet, and fixed it together.

Next, the boys were given the chance to rent a movie—but it was too expensive for a single group to pay for. After an intense negotiation, the Rattlers and Eagles pooled their money. That night, the boys agreed for the first time to sit together at dinner.

A few days later, all of the boys went on a camping trip, riding as Rattlers in one truck and Eagles in another. At the campsite, the researchers secretly broke down one of the trucks. The boys came together to pull on a rope to restart it, and celebrated together when they did. On their last night, the campers entertained each other around the campfire. They traveled home on one bus, sitting together, no longer separated into Rattlers and Eagles.

A shared goal can bring people together in extraordinary ways. It's used to build peace between warring countries, settle conflicts among groups, and negotiate compromises in relationships.

Right now, many of us are operating with an individual goal instead of a shared one. Remember from chapter 1 how you have an overarching goal that drives everything you do: your personal happiness.

Under the Old Happy worldview, your goal of *your* personal happiness is at odds with my goal of *my* personal happiness. For either one of us to be happy, we must beat the other person: I need to be better and achieve more and get more than you. Believing ourselves to be separate, we strive for personal happiness, even at others' expense.

But because we're connected, this doesn't work. It's like being in a three-legged race: when you're tied together, you need to move in the same direction or you'll fall. That's why we continually fall, again and again, dragging our fellow human beings through the mud.

This three-legged race is happening in bigger ways around the world, in cities, in countries, and in our relationship with nature. "No man chooses evil because it is evil," Mary Wollstonecraft, the writer, philosopher, and activist taught. "He only mistakes it for happiness, the good he seeks." Many people who are hurting others are not doing so intentionally, or even knowingly. They are doing it because they think it will lead to their personal happiness.

We are all tied together, in a twelve-billion-legged race, completely dependent on one another but pretending that we are not. What's the shared goal that will help us to move together?

Happiness—for everyone. A happier world.

Because now, you know: *my* happiness can only be satisfied by helping you with *your* happiness. When I use my gifts to help you, I become happy. And when you use your gifts to help me, you become happy.

In living by the New Happy philosophy, you are creating happiness not only for yourself, but also for others at the same time.

This shared goal allows us to put our arms around one another and move in the same direction, toward a world where everyone has what they need to be happy.

That is why Einstein said that the use of your gifts results in the "richest flourishing."

In these last chapters, we'll cover three ways you can start to share your gifts: through your work, in your community, and with the broader world.

Right now, somewhere up in space, astronauts are looking down on our planet. They might be experiencing the overview effect themselves, reflecting on our responsibility to one another. Maybe they're wondering, "How do we fix all of our problems?" They don't know that they're floating over you, someone who is about to start changing the world for the better.

KEY TAKEAWAYS

- In order to use our gifts to serve the world, we need to connect with the world.

- Start by abstracting your identity, from "you" to "a human being."

- Actively look for all of the ways the world helps you and contributes to your survival and well-being.

- For ultimate happiness, find a way to contribute to the world's well-being, too.

- When you live by the New Happy philosophy, you are not just working toward happiness for yourself. You are creating happiness for everyone.

15

Work:
The Perfect Job Nobody
Told You About

In 2013, the comedian John Oliver, a correspondent at *The Daily Show*, started a new project at work: a video series investigating how Australia implemented gun control laws. It was months after the Sandy Hook Elementary School shooting that killed twenty-six people, most of them six- and seven-year-old children.

As part of this project, Oliver interviewed Rob Borbidge, the former premiere of the state of Queensland, Australia. Borbidge was instrumental in passing gun control, although it came at a steep personal cost: he lost reelection and essentially ended his political career. Borbidge told Oliver that it didn't matter. He knew that he had done the right thing. "There are Australians alive today because we took that action," he said. "How much is a life worth?"

Oliver asked Borbidge how he defined success at work. He responded, "What makes a politician successful is that they're making society a better place."

Back in the United States, Oliver posed the exact same question to Jim Manley, a top aide to Harry Reid, a senator from Nevada. Manley's answer was quite different: "Success is getting reelected . . . if you don't get reelected, you're just roadkill in the political process, and you're just another loser."

Success is another one of those words, like *happiness*, that our worldview gloms onto and makes its own. The word itself doesn't actually define what success *is*. It simply means "to achieve a specific aim or purpose."

Under the Old Happy worldview, success is what Manley described: winning. Winning, as it turns out, is even more important than preventing kids and teachers from being killed in schools.

Old Happy teaches us to see work as a competition. We compete for the best jobs, and we strive to be the best at those jobs so we can get the next best job. Companies do anything they can to win in the market, even when it hurts people or the planet. The winners of this competition are hoisted onto pedestals, heralded as moral exemplars, even though the behavior that helped them win is often immoral. They are rewarded with money, power, influence, and the explicit right to dominate other people.

And those who lose or can't compete? Well, they just aren't good enough. They can't "make it" or "keep up with the pace here." We label them as *unsuccessful*, a designation that casts them as lesser beings and justifies all manner of horrors. (The fear that we, ourselves, will be branded as *unsuccessful* at our job drives us to overwork, leading to illness, disconnection, and unhappiness.)

The heartbreaking irony is that almost no one wants it to be this way.

REIMAGINE SUCCESS AT WORK

In one study, researchers set out to understand how people think about success. First, they asked participants to agree or disagree with a series of statements about how they believe other people define success. In response, 92 percent of people agreed that others view success as accumulating riches, fame, and power. Also, 86 percent agreed that others think that success can only be defined by comparing yourself to others.

Success isn't about beating others. It's about growing your own self.

Then the researchers asked them to agree or disagree to the same statements based on how they defined success *for themselves*. Of the participants, 97 percent agreed that success was pursuing their personal interests and talents (using your gifts). Also, 96 percent agreed that you can be successful regardless of how others do.

In short: we all think everyone else buys into Old Happy at work, but in reality, everyone wants New Happy. Real success is about using our gifts.

We are walking around believing the worst about one another and building institutions in that warped image, which is preventing us from using our gifts and, thus, blocking us from happiness. It doesn't have to be this way. We, the majority, want something different; we can speak up and enact change in our own workplaces, whether that is a 9-to-5, part-time work, seasonal work, a job you create, caregiving, or parenting.

Two powerful strategies can help you start using your gifts in your work: transform the existing job you have, or find a job that is a better fit for your gifts.

TRANSFORM THE JOB YOU HAVE

The intensive care unit is one of the most stressful workplaces in the world. The pace is fast, the hours are long, and the stakes are as high as they can be.

Thanh Neville, a pulmonologist, had been working at an intensive care unit for several years when she realized something: death was one of their common diagnoses. About one in five patients in critical care doesn't survive.

Neville later read in a journal about a Canadian hospital that implemented an initiative called the 3 Wishes Project (3WP), in which clinicians grant three end-of-life wishes for patients and their families. Neville realized that this could make a difference for her one in five patients and applied for a grant to implement it at her hospital.

The wishes vary, from a favorite meal to a bedside family gathering to bringing in Mickey Mouse. One of the nurses on the team had the idea to take fingerprints of the patients and make them into keychains. Neville told me, "Whenever I talk to a family member later, I ask them, 'Do you remember that keychain?' They hold it up and say, 'You mean this one, that I carry with me all of the time?'"

3WP brought together Neville's talent for medicine, her wisdom from the journal article and her work in the ICU, and her compassion. Implementing it changed her life for the better, she told me, describing a huge increase in her own sense of purpose and fulfillment. "It has brought me joy because I can do so much more for my patients now," she said, "and I have a much greater awareness that love is what matters most in life."

Neville told me a story about the first patient 3WP helped. He was a young man, in organ failure and on life support—married, just moved to Santa Monica, and loved the outdoors. His wife was horrified at the thought of him dying within the four walls of the hospital. The care team found a way to move him to a nearby patio. Neville gave his wife a blanket so she could crawl into bed with him. As the sun set, Neville disconnected his ventilator and he passed away. Every member of the staff was crying.

Four years later, Neville got an email from the hospital's development team about a large new donation coming in for 3WP. That young man's wife had gotten remarried, and she and her new husband had made this donation to help ensure other patients and families could have their wishes fulfilled, knowing how necessary help is in life's unbearable moments.

Neville was already helping through her work before starting 3WP, just like you are helping through your work already. She took it to the next level by crafting her job to use her gifts in new, fulfilling ways.

This is a strategy known as job-crafting, first proposed by the psychologists Amy Wrzesniewski and Jane Dutton. Studies have shown that job-crafting not only can make you happier and reduce your

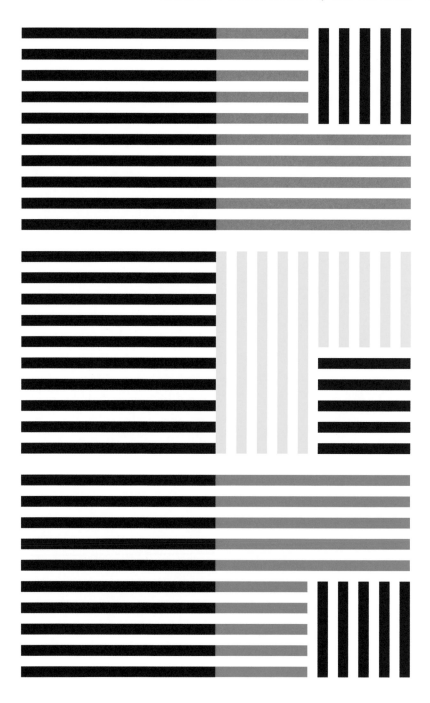

Rewrite your job description, crafting a role that uses your gifts.

stress, but even make you *better* at your work, even though you're not doing exactly what you're "supposed to do."

If job-crafting sounds intimidating, know that you're already doing it. As a completely unique person, you will always approach your work—whatever it is—in your own unique way.

You also have a lot of experience with crafting outside the workplace. For example:

- You wanted to start exercising. You started running on the treadmill but hated it, so you started cycling outside.
- You needed to take a business course to graduate. You signed up for an economic course but found it boring, so you switched to a marketing class.
- You wanted to be in a relationship. You didn't enjoy going to bars and clubs to meet people, so you signed up for a dating app instead.

There are always roadblocks that stand between us and our goals, and we are used to pivoting and finding new paths. *Crafting* is just another word for "creative problem-solving." In this case, you're taking the job you have and turning it into work that brings you joy.

Jobs are a mixture of the following activities:

- Required tasks: filing expenses, checking out customers, or restocking
- Ongoing tasks: weekly meetings, client reports, or sales calls
- Relationships: interactions with human beings like your colleagues, manager, or customers
- Projects: delivering a product, taking on a new market, rebranding, or taking on a case or client

The same holds true if your work is offered in a home:

- Required tasks: cleaning, feeding, or giving medicine
- Ongoing tasks: ordering supplies or scheduling appointments

- Relationships: connecting with the person or people you care for
- Projects: finding a new school for your child or getting a new treatment protocol started

Let's look at how to craft each of these.

Craft Your Tasks

In my research, I came across a story of a customer service representative from Chewy, a pet food company.

A woman named Anna, whose pet had just passed away, contacted Chewy to ask if she could return her unopened pet food. The representative gave her a full refund, told her to donate the food to a shelter, and then sent her a bouquet of flowers. When Anna posted about this experience online, many similar stories appeared: Chewy has a long track record of doing these kind things for their customers, even sometimes having paintings commissioned of dearly departed pets.

The people on this team had a task to do—responding to their customers' needs. But they did it in a way that used their humanity gifts: feeling compassion for their pain and taking the next loving action.

It's an equation: task × gift. How can you turn this task into something that helps you and others experience more happiness?

The next time you're at work, choose just one of your regular tasks and use this equation:

- Checking out customers × humanity = try to engage in a short but meaningful conversation with each person.
- Teaching a class × talent = weave your humor talent into the lecture, telling jokes to help your students remember key lessons.
- Writing status updates × wisdom = use your experience from past projects to anticipate questions and proactively answer them.

You also can use this strategy with all of your gifts—in this case, using the enhanced equation of task × gifts.

Michael Konstalid is a physical therapist, working in New York City's Department of Education, who helps kids with their mobility needs.

Konstalid has three unique gifts: the humanity from watching his father navigate a neuromuscular health condition, the wisdom of knowing how impactful specific accommodations can be, and the talent of carpentering that he learned from his dad. Konstalid realized that he could combine his gifts and create custom furniture for the children he works for, like crafting a seat for a child with a motor neuron disorder so that she could sit on the floor with her classmates.

In the first year of his job, he made eighty custom adaptive pieces—all free, all made from recycled or discarded furniture. He described the impact of making a piece for one particular child: "I see her in her class using something that I built, I know that I had a direct positive impact on her life and I know that her day is a little bit better, the light is shining a little bit brighter for her."

Craft Your Relationships

A friend of mine, Maria, works in data management. She didn't find her job enjoyable, but with young children at home, it wasn't a priority to find a new one. I suggested that she try to craft her job by focusing on using her humanity gifts to connect with her coworkers.

Maria, an introvert, started small. She decided that every time she got up from her desk, like to go to the bathroom or get a drink of water, she would stop and say hi to someone else. The first few times, people looked surprised to see her stopping by. Over time though, this action sparked relationships with people from across the company.

Within a few months, Maria became the "go-to" person at the company, thanks to her new web of connections. She expressed her surprise that such a simple practice could make such a big difference:

"I truly enjoy going to work now, and while my daily tasks haven't changed, it feels like a completely new job. It's even made me a better mother and partner."

Take a cue from Maria by starting to use your humanity gifts in your daily work life. In your next interaction or meeting, can you tap into your humanity and take the next loving action?

Craft a Project

A few years ago, the principal at West Side Elementary School in Healdsburg, California, made a call to Jessica Martin, an artist specializing in mixed-media art. The principal wanted to know if she would come to the school and start a brand-new arts program. Martin was apprehensive but decided to take the leap. Within two weeks, she had fallen head over heels for the students, teachers, and community.

In 2020, Martin was contemplating how she could teach her students about compassion. She connected with a fellow teacher named Asherah Weiss, and together they came up with the idea of creating a "compassion hotline."

Martin and Weiss asked their students questions about compassion and recorded their answers for the hotline, which they named Peptoc. If you can, I urge you, right now, to call this number to hear it for yourself: 1-707-873-7862. Callers are given a menu of options: If you're feeling mad, frustrated, or nervous, press 1. If you need words of encouragement and life advice, press 2. If you need a pep talk, press 3.

If you press 2, you'll hear recorded voices from children encouraging you to keep going:

"Be grateful for yourself."

"Dude, live it up!"

"Be YOU!"

"It's okay to be different."

"The world is a better place with you in it."

Peptoc quickly went viral, receiving more than five million calls in the three months after it launched.

No one put "design a hotline" in Martin's and Weiss's job descriptions. You, too, can come up with a project that brings you joy and makes an impact on the world. Brainstorm by asking yourself these questions:

- If I was in charge of this company, what project would I launch?
- What project would make my work more fun or meaningful?
- How do I think we could better support the people we serve?

Make your work work for *you*, and everyone benefits.

In talking to Martin about Peptoc, I discovered something that gave me goosebumps: her inspiration for the project came from her friend, the artist Susan O'Malley, whom we met in chapter 13. Jessica wanted to help carry out O'Malley's dream of a more loving world; in the process, she helped millions of people herself. Look at how using your gifts ripples outward in ways you will never imagine.

FIND A NEW JOB THAT USES YOUR GIFTS

After fifteen years working at Nike, where he oversaw the golf and tennis shoe division, Jesse Milliken was feeling restless. He didn't know what he wanted, but he knew he wanted more. As he was grappling with these emotions, he was also watching the terrifying flames engulfing his home state of Oregon. It made him realize that he wanted to use his gifts to address climate change.

He thought about the talents he had developed while at Nike: designing shoes, managing supply chain, and launching products. His

Seek out a new environment that will give you the room to grow.

wife, Megan, had extensive wisdom from her career in corporate sustainability. Perhaps, he wondered, they could work together on something.

One day, it hit him, a gift of wisdom: he thought about his three children and all of the clothes they so quickly outgrew. As it turns out, 183 million pieces of outgrown children's clothing are thrown into landfills every year. They could do something about this.

The Millikens started a company called Woolybubs, starting off with environmentally friendly baby shoes. Normal baby shoes take between fifty and a thousand years to break down in landfills, but Woolybubs's can be boiled in water and completely dissolved in less than forty-five minutes.

There might be times in your life when you, like Milliken, feel that you need more from your work. I know it can be difficult, but it is also something to celebrate. It's a sign that you're ready to become an even greater version of yourself.

When you are growing a plant, you start it in a small pot. With care and attention, that plant begins to grow bigger and its roots expand within the soil. If you're not careful, your plant will become root-bound, and the roots will no longer be able to get nutrients from the soil. This can lead to the plant withering and even dying.

As you use your gifts, you will grow in a similar way. Eventually, your roots will expand as far as they can go, which means that you need to plant yourself in a new, bigger pot.

Think of it this way: your job is not your *work*. Your true work is being yourself and giving of yourself—that's what real success is all about. Your job is just one place that is helping you do that right now. When it stops helping you do that, continue growing by finding a new job that helps you continue doing your work (or by finding new ways to grow and contribute outside it, as we'll discuss in the next two chapters).

Never make a job the thing you give your highest loyalty to. Your highest loyalty must always be to the work of being and giving yourself.

You can make a habit to check in with yourself, asking, "Is this job helping me be myself and give of myself?" If the answer is no (and remains no consistently), that's a sign to find a new pot where you can expand your roots and keep growing.

How do you do it?

Journalists are taught to use the "5Ws and 1H of journalism," which helps them identify the who, what, when, where, why, and how of a story.

To help you find or make a job that uses your gifts, you can use this same framework, too:

- What: What gifts do you most want to use? Choose the gifts that feel the most enjoyable or meaningful to you right now. Pay special attention to your wisdom and humanity gifts, which often get overlooked at work.
- Where: Where might your gifts be valued and appreciated? Identify industries or roles that would benefit from all that you are, know, and can do. Challenge yourself to think beyond your current environment.
- Why: Is there a greater "why?" you'd like to address, as Milliken did with climate change?
- Who: Whom do you know who could help you explore these opportunities (a personal connection, an online resource, an expert in the field, a mentor, or even a stranger)?
- How: How will you take action?
- When: When will you do it?

Changing jobs can be an overwhelming experience. This tool can help: not only does it break the process into achievable steps, but it also keeps you aligned to your personal definition of success.

PUT GIVING AT THE CENTER

When Jelani Memory was in high school, he was nominated for "Most Likely to Be Father of the Year."

Twenty years later, he has founded a children's publishing company, called A Kids Co. The books Memory publishes have a specific aim: to help kids have important and empowering conversations with the grown-ups in their lives, covering topics from empathy to school shootings to failure to illness to divorce to death. The company has sold millions of books, and in the process, helped facilitate millions of better conversations between caregivers and children.

At fourteen, Memory became an uncle when his first niece was born. He was surprised by how much he loved being an uncle and how naturally it came to him. Memory hadn't had a father figure himself; his dad left their family when he was four years old. He told me, "Hearing about a kid who had a dad that played basketball with them in the yard, that was like a dispatch from another planet." His mom, a nurse, had to work constantly to support their family, and they rarely had time for the important conversations about fears or feelings or frustrations.

Memory grew up. He made his own family. He started his own company, Circle Media, where he used his marketing and leadership talents to help parents manage their kids' screen time.

One day, he thought about a conversation he wanted to have with his kids about racism. He spent a week writing down his stories, insights, and guidance for his children. Printing just one copy, he chose a title: *A Kids Book About Racism*. He showed it to his kids, and their first response was, "Dad, you need to make more!"

Their reaction is what inspired Memory to start A Kids Co. It turns out that his classmates were right—partially. He wasn't only meant to be Father of the Year. He was meant to be the person *helping other parents* be Parent of the Year in their own homes.

Memory told me how important it was that he put giving at the center of everything he does, sharing, "I have tried to give as much as

I can in every domain of my life. I think constantly about how to do it in my work life, my community life, my relational life, and in my life with my kids."

I asked him, "How has living in this way affected your happiness?"

His response was decisive: "It has had a monumental impact on my life. I'm naturally depressive, naturally sad, naturally cynical. When I'm giving, I'm instantly fueled with joy and energy. It has changed everything."

No matter what you do for work, Memory's wisdom can serve as a powerful guide. Much of what happens at work falls outside of our control. What is always within our control, though, is the way we choose to look at it. Like Memory describes, we can learn to see our work as a place where we *get* to give. With this perspective, daily tasks and interactions can be transformed into moments of joy.

As it turns out, work is perfectly positioned to be a source of happiness: it is a prime example of our interdependence, a place that enables constant giving and receiving. That beautiful cake your friends surprised you with on your birthday? It was the result of the staff at your local bakery's incredible talents. That national park you visited this summer, where you felt awe and built lifelong memories? It's lovingly managed by a group of government employees and volunteers. The painting that adorns your wall, the television show that made you weep with laughter, the bicycle that you ride on the weekends—they're all the result of other people's gifts at work.

It's your turn to share your gifts with others. When you do, you'll know for yourself that it's the greatest form of success there is.

KEY TAKEAWAYS

- You can reject Old Happy's definition of success and define it for yourself.

- Work is the perfect place to start sharing your gifts with the world.

- Craft your job by: applying the task × gift equation, using your humanity gifts in your work relationships, and taking on projects that use your gifts.

- If you need a new environment to keep expanding, use the "5Ws and 1H" tool to brainstorm new roles and possibilities.

- Keep giving at the heart of your work and you will always be successful.

16

Community:
The Common Threads
That Connect Us

One night, Haraldur Thorleifsson went out for a walk with his wife and two young children in downtown Reykjavik, Iceland. His three-year-old son was thirsty, so they found a corner store where he could get something to drink. But Thorleifsson couldn't join them inside. The store entrance had a step, and he uses a wheelchair.

While his family was inside, he sat alone outside. As he told me, "I thought about all of the times I've had to sit outside while my family goes to do something. And I thought about all of the times I've missed out on meeting my friends because the café or restaurant wasn't accessible. And I thought about how, over time, people who use wheelchairs will stop trying to go out because it's heartbreaking to keep running into these obstacles constantly, so we slowly fade out of normal life."

At the time, Thorleifsson was a design leader at Twitter and had recently moved back home to Iceland. In his frequent travels, he had seen that countries had the power to make their cities accessible. Many just chose not to.

He decided to start a program called Ramp Up Iceland that would build one hundred ramps in downtown Reykjavik. They completed these ramps in seven months, fundamentally changing the culture of the city. Stories poured in of people sharing that they could go downtown in their wheelchairs for the first time in decades or visit the restaurant that they had always wanted to try. Now, Ramp Up is going even bigger: building fifteen hundred ramps across Iceland.

Thorleifsson's story serves as an example for how you, too, can start using your gifts in your communities.

WHY WE NEED TO CARE FOR OUR COMMONS

A few hundred years ago, a writer named William Forster Lloyd published a pamphlet describing what happens to a common good that is shared, like a piece of land where cattle herders let their cows graze. He argued that people will make decisions that benefit their self interest—in this case, letting more of their cattle graze on the shared field. In the long term, this behavior leads to overgrazing and the destruction of the field itself. Everyone ends up losing.

In the 1960s, an ecologist (and, as it turns out, eugenicist) named Garrett Hardin picked up on Lloyd's work and popularized it, calling it "the tragedy of the commons." He believed that people cannot be trusted to manage resources on their own, arguing that there are only two solutions: privatizing property (which gives someone a financial incentive to care for it) or government control (which allows them to set regulations on it).

The tragedy of the commons has persisted as a belief, even though it's inaccurate—something that the political scientist Elinor Ostrom discovered (and won the Nobel Prize for in 2009). Ostrom didn't buy into Hardin's pessimistic view of human beings' selfishness. She went out into local communities where they were managing common resources and tried to understand what they were doing differently. Along the way, she discovered that it is possible for us to care for the collective in a way where everyone benefits.

Ostrom focused on natural resources, like forests and fisheries. I

When we take from the commons, they are diminished. When we use our gifts to contribute to the commons, they are enriched.

have long thought that her insights also apply to the way we care for all of our commons—like the communities where people gather, which belong to everyone and extend belonging to everyone.

CLAIM YOUR COMMUNITIES

Everywhere I turn, I see people who are hungry to know that they matter, that they are needed, and that they are a part of a greater community.

To belong is one of our core human needs, associated with benefits as diverse as mental and physical health, better relationships, and achievement. Research shows that living in a community with a high level of trust contributes to your personal happiness. People with strong community ties are significantly happier than those with weak ones. It even makes you more resilient: following natural disasters, trusting communities report fewer psychological challenges and bounce back far more quickly.

You belong to many communities already. You might just take them for granted.

You are a part of not only the great web of human connectedness, but also many groups within that: your town or city; your cycling club or knitting circle; your temple, church, mosque, or gurdwara; your yoga studio or dog park; your group chat; your mutual aid group; your social media community. There are threads connecting you to so many others and groups around you.

The first step to greater belonging is claiming the communities that we are already a part of. It's as simple as looking around and saying, "That's my support group," or "That's my neighborhood," or "That's my library," or "That's my school." In doing so, we set ourselves up not to abandon the commons, but to care for them.

In one study, researchers planted garbage on the surface of a lake where kayakers would go out paddling. When kayakers went to rent a boat, they were asked if they wanted to participate in a short experiment. If they said yes, half of them were told to think of a nickname for the lake before going out on it. Of the people who nicknamed the

You are already a part of many communities that need you.
Claim them, connect with them, and contribute to them.

lake, 41 percent tried to pick up the trash; of those who didn't, only 6 percent did.

Claiming something creates a sense of psychological ownership, which transforms the way that you perceive and treat that something. It helps us shift from looking at communities and thinking, "Someone should do something about that," to thinking, "That's my community; I can do something about that."

This is exactly what Thorleifsson did. He claimed Reykjavik for his own and took responsibility for it. He made himself the someone.

YOU ARE THE PERSON YOUR COMMUNITY NEEDS

When you were a child, did you ever play in a ball pit? It's a large, padded play space that's filled with hundreds of colorful plastic balls.

The big problems in our world—climate change, racism, health, poverty—are each like their own separate ball pits. Within them, the plastic balls represent the way this problem is being expressed in local communities.

The big pit of "make the world accessible" is filled with many different plastic balls labeled "make Reykjavik accessible," "make Los Angeles accessible," and "make Mumbai accessible," as well as other plastic balls like "ensure workplace disability rights," "increase representation in media," and "make products accessible."

Thorleifsson reached into the pit and plucked out the ball that affected his local community, where he had grown up, where he had existing relationships, where he knew the culture and the needs. It was the ball that he could do something about. As he told me, "The world is the way it is because someone decided it should be that way. That means you can decide it should be different."

This is a key principle of Elinor Ostrom's research. The best way to solve local problems is by having local people use their gifts to come up with local solutions. We can follow in Thorleifsson's footsteps, and if we do, eventually, all of the plastic balls will be removed.

In my research, I came across a story about how Mexico City put this principle into action. The city has a population of nine million people, of which 70 percent use the public bus service, which offers fourteen million rides every day. But despite that, there were no maps for the bus routes. People in Mexico City had to figure out, from a friend or family member or neighbor, how to travel through the city to get to where they wanted to go.

The mayor of Mexico City established a think tank within the government called *Laboratorio para la Ciudad* (Laboratory for the City), led by Gabriella Gómez-Mont, a journalist, artist, and documentarian. When he brought her this problem, she had a gift of wisdom to share: the greatest strength that they had was the citizens of Mexico City. If there was a way to bring them together and tap into their collective gifts, perhaps they could solve this problem.

The *Laboratorio* created a digital game and invited citizens to play as they took the bus: they could "map out" the specific route they took and earn points that could be exchanged for different rewards. Their maps then fed into an open database that city planners could use to chart the bus routes. More than four thousand citizens participated and a full map of the bus system was completed in just two weeks.

A traditional mapping approach, run by outsiders, would have cost many millions of dollars. The *Laboratorio*'s approach? It cost less than $15,000.

Too often, community members downplay or dismiss their unique gifts, thinking that they have nothing special to offer. That couldn't be further from the truth. With your humanity, talent, and wisdom, who could be better suited? You are the very best person to help solve the problems in your community. You just need to find the place where your gifts are needed.

WHERE IS HAPPINESS BEING THWARTED?

Lisa Thomas-McMillan has spent most of her life helping people who are hungry. She once walked 115 miles from her home in Brewton, Alabama, to the governor in Montgomery, hand-delivering a letter explaining why they needed to provide more support for hungry people. Then she decided that wasn't enough and kept walking all the way to Washington, DC. It took her fifty-three days. Her humanity gifts are very strong.

One day, Thomas-McMillan read a story about Jon Bon Jovi's restaurant, JBJ Soul Kitchen, that gives away free meals to anyone who is hungry. It sparked something in her: that is what she wanted to do, too.

In 2018, she and her husband, Freddie, used their gifts to fulfill this lifelong dream and opened Drexel & Honeybee's, a donation-only restaurant in downtown Brewton, Alabama. She used her extraordinary talents as a chef; he lovingly refurbished the building from scratch.

Everyone eats, no matter what you can pay. At the front of the restaurant, there's a donation box where you can contribute if you have the means or want to help cover the costs of feeding others. Thomas-McMillan says that, often, they get notes in the box, saying: "If it wasn't for this restaurant, I wouldn't have eaten today."

Residents of Brewton were skeptical about her restaurant at first; now, it attracts tourists from all over the country, looking to see Thomas-McMillan's gifts in action. As she told me, "It's the best feeling in the world to get up in the morning and get out into that restaurant and start fixing food." She acknowledges that it isn't always easy, but she says it is always joyful. "Even when I get frustrated or tired, the joy is always there for me. It's the ultimate happiness."

Thomas-McMillan's story reminds us that every person's happiness is dependent upon a broader set of commons: safety and security; housing, food, and water; access to institutions like schools and hospitals; economic opportunity and stability; support systems; and the freedom to be yourself. When people don't have these things, their happiness is being thwarted.

Today, as you interact with your communities, look for the places where happiness is being thwarted—for that is where your gifts may be needed.

Are there people in your community who are . . .

- Hungry, unsheltered, unsafe, or ill?
- Struggling to find a job, attend school, or work with institutions?
- Feeling lonely or isolated?
- Unable to access resources or support?
- Experiencing discrimination or persecution?

Caring for the commons means finding ways to fulfill these needs for the people around you, knowing that people thrive when they have the support that they need.

Another powerful example comes from Keyatta Mincey Parker, an award-winning craft bartender in Atlanta. When the pandemic hit, she watched as millions from the hospitality community were laid off around the country, including many of her friends and coworkers.

A few months earlier, Mincey Parker had secured a quarter acre of land in Atlanta, hoping to start a garden where she could use the gifts that she learned from her grandmother and mother in Liberia. She quickly realized that this garden could be used to support her community members, many of whom were struggling to pay their bills and cope with the challenges of the pandemic.

She named the garden A Sip of Paradise and opened it up as a community garden for the Atlanta bartending community. "I wanted a place where I could play in the dirt with my friends," she told me. "The garden was an opportunity for people to come and be themselves, to vent, to get away, to get out of the house, put their phone down." It's since expanded into a full nonprofit: they have movement and mindfulness classes, guest bartender events, and a database to help their members find better jobs.

Mincey Parker, knowing herself to be "the someone," saw that happiness was being thwarted for her community members and offered to help. This choice helped her, too: "It's beautiful to see the impact that we have in our community. My mental space is a lot better.

Because I'm actually doing things that I enjoy. I'm happy because I'm doing good things with my friends."

You don't have to open a restaurant or start a garden to care for your commons. It can be a small, daily habit. A friend of mine, Brian, lives in Los Angeles. He has been passionate about the environment since he was a child. He cites his mother as the one who taught him to love and care for nature, telling me, "I learned that if you love nature, then it's extremely important to protect it." For many of us, the trash on the side of the road has become invisible. But not to Brian. On his nightly walks with his wife, he brings along a trash pickup stick and an empty garbage bag and fills the bag as they walk.

WHAT CAN WE DO TOGETHER?

Thirty years ago, the tiny town of Colquitt, Georgia, was struggling.

The local sewing factory had shut down, jobs were disappearing, and people were moving away. In the words of one resident, Joy Jinks, it was felt like a dying town: stores boarded up, empty parking spaces, and streets empty of people. No one knew what to do.

One day, Jinks happened to meet a doctoral student in theater studies named Richard Geer, who had a big, bold idea: he believed that the arts could heal communities.

What if, Geer wondered, we gathered the real stories of the Colquitt community and turned them into a musical? Could it save the town?

With nothing to lose, Jinks invited Geer to test out his big idea in Colquitt. They called the show *Swamp Gravy* in honor of a meal that residents would cook on the side of the creek while fishing.

The residents were skeptical, to say the least. As the fire chief said, "Why would people pay money to come see stories they already know?"

The night of the performance, as the curtain rose, Joy sat anxiously alongside many of her fellow residents in the audience, completely unsure what to expect.

Swamp Gravy was a hit. The performers felt energized and empowered; the audience felt seen and validated; the community came together, bonded by the show.

Now, thirty years later, *Swamp Gravy* is still running, an annual performance that has completely transformed Colquitt. Not only has it provided the residents with numerous ways to share their unique gifts, but it also has revitalized the town itself: people show up by the thousands to see their annual performance, bringing in more than $7 million a year in tourism spending. With the revenue, the town built a beautiful performance hall and provided communal resources for the town. The *Swamp Gravy* cast was invited to perform at the Kennedy Center in Washington, DC, and at the 1996 Atlantic Olympics.

People aren't leaving Colquitt the way they used to; they're staying and contributing to the community. People are even moving there to contribute to *Swamp Gravy*, like this stage manager who described their experience as the most fulfilling experience of their lives, providing them with something they had always been looking for but never been able to find: a true community of people who take care of each other.

When a community comes together, using their unique gifts in pursuit of a common goal, extraordinary things happen. Look around for where people in your community are doing good. How can you join them? They might need someone who knows how to make websites, or someone who has a talent for design to make flyers, or someone who is connected to a specific temple. They might be looking for a person who is great with kids, or who is a public speaker, or who has a free Saturday that they're willing to use to help clean the beach. They might need you.

Here's a script you can use to reach out to these organizations:

> I'm looking to contribute to my community. I admire the
> work you and your team are doing to solve [problem],

which is something that I feel very passionately about, too. I have a few gifts that I can share: [describe your gifts]. If I can be of service to your organization's goals, it would be great to learn more about how I can get involved.

If you don't see your community gathering, you now know your role: be the one who brings people together, just like Geer and Jinks did.

There are people in your community who are just waiting for the chance to use their gifts. Think about the residents of Colquitt, none of whom would have ever been given the chance to shine on a stage without *Swamp Gravy*. Everyone was welcome because everyone had something meaningful to share. Geer would tell everyone at auditions that they had to pass a very important test: he would hold up a mirror to their mouth and, if it fogged up, they were welcome in the cast.

In a paper describing the project, Geer wrote about how astounded he had been by the depth of wisdom that lived within each member of the theatre company and how, when they were given the opportunity to express it, it could transform both that individual and the broader community. In seeking to help the residents of Colquitt, Geer had to admit that, in reality, it was they who had helped him.

YOUR COMMUNITY NEEDS
YOUR COMPASSION

Katie Steller is a hair salon owner in Minneapolis. As a child, she had severe ulcerative colitis, leading her to spend much of her youth in and out of hospitals. The disease made her hair very thin, and one day her mom took her to get a professional haircut to make her feel a little bit better. This inspired her to become a hair stylist herself, hoping to offer the same experience to others.

A few years ago, Steller was struggling with her mental health while opening her salon. As she told me, "I was having a wave of hopelessness and depression about the world, and feeling so overwhelmed by all of the pain in it."

You do not have to understand exactly how someone is feeling.
You just need to be there for them and help however you can.

Then she looked around her living room and noticed all of the big red salon chairs that were sitting there, waiting to be installed at the salon. It inspired her. She asked herself, "Okay, what can I do? I can't fix it all, but I can do something."

She thought of the many people experiencing homelessness whom she drove past every day. Normally, this thought would make her feel even more despairing, but today, she was determined to respond in a different way. Purposefully, she walked out of the house and drove toward her salon, stopping by a man whom she passed every day. She stopped, asked him his name, and then said, "Hey, do you want a free haircut? I can go grab my salon stuff and do it right here." His name was Edward, and he laughed and told her that he had a funeral to go to the next day, and he would love a haircut.

As you start caring for the community, you will likely encounter a lot of suffering. Sometimes, like Steller experienced, it can feel overwhelming. You might even feel an impulse to pull away from it or ignore it.

If we want to belong and create belonging for others, we need to learn a different response.

This instinct to distance is, in fact, the result of one of our natural strengths of empathy. When you empathize with someone, you are quite literally sharing their feelings. The part of your brain that feels pain activates when you see someone else in pain. This can lead to overwhelming feelings of personal distress, leaving you completely ill-equipped or physically unable to help those who need it most. You become self-focused. (If you've ever been sad, told a loved one about it, and then somehow found yourself comforting *them*, you know what this is like.)

We can evolve our instinctive empathy into compassion, which is the state that motivates and empowers us to help others. Compassion involves feeling loving, positive emotions toward a person, coupled with the desire to alleviate their pain. It's other-focused.

In one study, the Buddhist monk and philosopher Matthieu Ricard was asked to look at photos of children who were suffering and describe the different experiences of empathy and compassion.

With empathy, he said: "The empathic sharing of their pain very quickly became intolerable to me and I felt emotionally exhausted, very similar to being burned out."

With compassion, he described it quite differently: "Although the images of the suffering children were still as vivid as before, they no longer induced distress. Instead, I felt natural and boundless love for these children and the courage to approach and console them."

This is a remarkable discovery: you can be present with people who are suffering in a way that doesn't lead to your own suffering, but that instead fills you with positive, loving feelings and equips you to help them. Shifting from empathy to compassion is an essential skill for being in community with one another.

To evolve your empathy into compassion, think back to that image you learned in chapter 11: the house inside of you that is filled with light. Picture allowing that light to shine on the person in front of you.

You don't need to take on their pain or suffering because that will make you a less effective helper. You don't need to fix them because they are not broken. You just need to love the person in front of you and use that love to guide the next actions that you take.

That's exactly what Steller did. Since that day, she has been traveling around Minneapolis on her days off with a big red salon chair, giving haircuts. Edward became her longest-standing client and friend. She's building the community she wants to belong to by extending belonging in the ways she can.

In caring for your community's suffering, you end up alleviating it. That's why Coretta Scott King said, "The greatness of a community is most accurately measured by the compassionate actions of its members."

KEY TAKEAWAYS

- You are already a part of many communities. Claim them, and make yourself the "someone."

- People within communities are the best equipped to solve their local challenges.

- Look for the needs within your communities and ways you can address them. Ask yourself, "Where is happiness being thwarted?"

- When you encounter pain in your communities, practice shifting from empathy to compassion.

17

World:
We're Waiting for You

The chef and restauranteur José Andrés lives in Washington, DC, but you're far more likely to find him on the front lines of a war or a disaster, feeding people nourishing meals in the worst moments of their lives.

As a young man, Andrés was a chef in the Spanish navy and traveled to countries where there was extreme hunger, an experience that led to several of his gifts: the motivation to ensure no person goes hungry and the talent to feed them.

After immigrating to the United States, he started volunteering at a nonprofit addressing hunger called DC Central Kitchen, founded by a nightclub manager and his now-mentor, Robert Egger. Inspired by Egger's wisdom, Andrés started his own nonprofit, World Central Kitchen, which has now fed millions of people affected by disasters all over the world.

When Puerto Rico was devastated by Hurricane Maria, Andrés got on the first commercial flight, planning to stay and cook for a few days. His team quickly scaled up, gathering twenty thousand volunteers who ended up cooking and serving more than four million meals. Within twenty-four hours of Russia's invasion of Ukraine, World Central Kitchen was on site, handing out warm food to the millions of women and children rushing over the border. Wherever there are people devastated, World Central Kitchen wants to be there to help them. "We have one mission and one very simple objective," Andrés says: "Feed the hungry, bring water to the thirsty."

WE ARE AN ORCHESTRA

Some of us are called to serve in our work; others in our communities; and some, like Andrés, on a global level. Whatever way you choose to help, it all adds up.

You do not need to fix the world all by yourself. In fact, you *can't*.

There is absolutely no problem that can be solved by one person. That's an Old Happy myth, grounded in individualism, the idea that there's a single hero coming to save us. Even those operating at the greatest scale, like Andrés, are only able to do so because they are enabled by so many others: tens of thousands of volunteers, local restaurants and food providers, grants, and donations.

Making our world better is not a soloist task. It is an orchestral one.

In an orchestra, every instrument—the violin, the trombone, the oboe, the bass, the harp, the timpani, the cello—is needed. Were you to hear just one instrument playing its part in a symphony alone, it wouldn't make sense because it was detached from the greater whole. The beauty is in the way all of the unique parts come together.

Our orchestra is incomplete without you. We need you to play the part that only you can play.

Look around you and ask yourself, "What is the problem that I most want to see solved in the world?"

You might have an immediate answer to this question. If you do, it probably comes from your gifts.

- Humanity: From a moment when you were moved by another person's suffering.
- Wisdom: From the experiences you went through or learned from.

The world's problems are too big for one person to solve alone.
If we bring all of our gifts together, we can build a better world.

- Talent: From the skills you have gained that have a particular application, like medicine or research.

We have also created a list of the problems that the world needs your help with. See if there is a specific one on this sample list that calls to you:

Health:
- Mental health
- Infectious diseases (HIV/ AIDS, malaria, Lyme, COVID-19, etc.)
- Noninfectious diseases (cancer, Alzheimer's, etc.)
- Affordable health care
- Health-care equity

Violence:
- War
- Land mines
- Disarmament
- Gun violence

Rights and representation:
- Racism and racial injustice
- Discrimination
- Gender equality
- LGBTQIA+ rights
- Rights of disabled people
- Voting rights
- Reproductive rights

Access:
- Education
- Immigration
- Housing
- Drinking water

Economic:
- Poverty
- Better workplaces
- Homelessness
- Quality jobs

Planet:
- Restoration
- Fossil fuels
- Food access
- Species extinction
- Forest protection
- Sustainable agriculture
- Ocean pollution
- Plastic waste

Society:
- Aging
- Addiction
- Loneliness
- Supporting refugees

The full list is available at thenewhappy.com/theproblems.

(Whatever problem you choose, you'll notice immediately that they all can also be addressed through your work and in your community. Remember the ball pit: sometimes the best thing you can do is to pluck one plastic ball out of the bigger problem pit.)

Each of us will have our own unique way to help with the world's problems. For example, let's consider three different people and how they are using their gifts to address climate change.

In South Africa, Sam Alfred is a video game designer. He lived in Cape Town during the city's 2018 water crisis, when they nearly ran out of water. He created a video game called *Terra Nil*, which guides players through the rejuvenation of a ravaged environment.

In Singapore, the artist Tan Zi Xi gathered more than twenty-six thousand pieces of plastic from the ocean for a museum installation, hanging every piece from the walls and the ceiling to demonstrate what it feels like to live in an environment that is surrounded by garbage.

And in Indonesia, Mina Susana Setra is an Indigenous activist who has been fighting for climate change since her home was converted to a palm oil plantation. She has helped implement multiple policies and created a television channel that provides a way for marginalized communities to speak up about their experiences.

Alfred, Zi Xi, and Setra aren't waiting for someone else to solve the problem that matters to them. They are doing what they can, right here and now. I know, when you look at them, you don't expect them to solve climate change all by themselves! Don't expect that of yourself either. That belief keeps you from taking any action at all.

So many inspiring people have used their gifts to help solve the world's problems. Through their stories, we can learn seven key lessons to guide us in our own journeys:

1. Be a role model.
2. Change where you share your gifts.
3. Reject the way it's always been done.
4. Fight for what is right.
5. Hope builds with action.
6. Embrace the challenge.
7. Dream big; start small.

LESSON #1:
BE A ROLE MODEL

In 1964, the actress Nichelle Nichols became one of the first Black women to be cast in a lead role on a television show, starring in the role of Lieutenant Uhura on *Star Trek*.

After the first season, Nichols decided she wanted to leave the show to pursue her dreams of performing on Broadway. She told Gene Roddenberry, the creator, about her intention, and he begged her to think it over on the weekend before making a final decision. As it happened, that weekend she was attending an NAACP fundraiser in Beverly Hills when someone tapped her on the shoulder and said, "Nichelle, there's a fan here who wants to meet you."

It was Martin Luther King Jr. He was a huge Trekkie, thrilled by the vision of an egalitarian world that it painted for its viewers.

In their conversation, Nichols told him that she was planning on leaving the show. King told her that she absolutely could not do that. He beseeched her to focus on what she had achieved in her role on the show, telling her, "For the first time, we are being seen the world over as we should be seen." It was the only show, he told her, that his little children were allowed to stay up late to watch.

Nichols decided to stay. King showed her that she had an important role in the civil rights movement, using her gifts to serve as a role model for millions of Black girls, women, and people. This representation is critical: in one recent study, Black female students who were studying STEM topics (science, technology, engineering, and math)

By using your gifts, you lead the way and show what's possible.

felt a greater sense of belonging if they had access to Black female role models in the field. When Nichols looked back on her role as Uhura, she said, "It makes me feel that it's worthy being in this business, because you can touch other people before you even meet them in good ways."

Because Nichols stayed on the show, she ended up having a positive impact upon so many—even inspiring the first Black woman in space, Mae Jemison, who adored *Star Trek*. When Jemison was aboard the *Endeavor* on a 1992 mission, she honored her role model every time she opened communications by using Lieutenant Uhura's signature phrase: "Hailing frequencies open."

To be who you are and to boldly go where you have never gone before—this is an act of service. It gives other people the courage to follow their dreamed-of paths, too. We all need someone who shows us, "Here I am being me; you can be you, too."

LESSON #2:
CHANGE WHERE YOU SHARE YOUR GIFTS

Shigeru Ban is one of the most celebrated architects in the world. Although he does design award-winning museums and monuments, he cares much more about the temporary shelters he builds for victims of natural disasters and wars.

In 1985, Ban was assisting on an exhibit for another architect and trying to figure out how to display the work with no money to spend on any fancy materials. He gathered his used sketch paper and formed it into paper tubes, a chance innovation that would end up changing his life.

These paper tubes are surprisingly strong, environmentally friendly, and inexpensive. Immediately following the Rwandan genocide in 1994, Ban proposed using these tubes to create temporary shelters for those fleeing the country. Since then, he has devoted himself to designing sustainable shelters for tens of thousands of people who have been affected by earthquakes, tsunamis, and disasters all around the world. His most recent shelter, designed to help the millions of people left homeless by the 2023 earthquakes in Turkey and Syria, takes just five minutes to assemble.

Ban says he started working to help disaster victims because he was disappointed in his own profession. He said, "We're working for privileged people who have money and power. I hope to use my knowledge and experiences not only for privilege, but for the general public."

You might be used to sharing your gifts in one specific place or way. But as Ban's story shows, we all can think creatively and find new ways to use our gifts to help those who need it most. Scan through the earlier list of problems and ask yourself, "Where might my gifts be needed? How could I be useful?"

LESSON #3:
REJECT THE WAY IT'S ALWAYS BEEN DONE

In upstate New York, there's a man running a billion-dollar corporation who is known as the anti-CEO.

Hamdi Ulukaya immigrated to the United States from Turkey in 1994, working on a farm and taking English classes. Later, he started a business that imported cheeses from Turkey, but it was a struggle. A few years in, a nearby yogurt factory went up for sale. Ulukaya wondered if Americans would enjoy the yogurt he had grown up making on his family's farm—a thick, creamy product that wasn't widely available. Using a loan, he purchased the factory and launched the company that we know as Chobani.

From the beginning, Ulukaya was determined to do things differently. He believes that businesses have an obligation to help humanity.

He's demonstrated this through his commitment to helping refugees. After hearing that there were local refugees who couldn't find jobs, he hired them and created a work environment to support them: bringing in translators, setting up training, and arranging for their

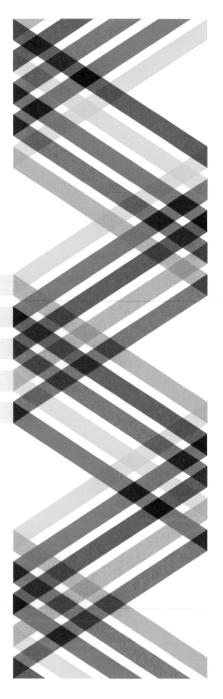

Question the way it's always been done; we can always do better.

transportation to work. He launched a program called the Tent Partnership for Refugees and got three hundred companies to commit to hiring refugees.

Follow in Ulukaya's footsteps, and reject the status quo. As you start to use your gifts to serve the world, you might encounter resistance from other people. They might tell you, "That won't work," or "This is how it's always been done." Reject these limiting perspectives. A better way is *always* possible.

LESSON #4:
FIGHT FOR WHAT IS RIGHT

In 2014, a Microsoft engineer named Matt Hite stumbled onto a nonprofit called Warfighter Engaged, which provides wounded and disabled veterans with modified equipment to play video games.

Hite reached out, learning from the founder that most controllers require heavy manual adaptation to suit disabled people's needs. There are more than a billion people with disabilities around the world, and Microsoft wasn't giving them a product they could actually use.

Inspired, Hite gathered a team of people to participate in Microsoft's 2015 Hackathon, kicking off an extraordinary series of events. Although Hite's project didn't move forward, it did inspire another employee at Microsoft named Bryce Johnson, an accessibility leader.

A year later, in the 2016 Hackathon, Johnson gathered a new team to tackle this problem again. This time, an executive agreed to devote resources to the project. Johnson's team started working with Warfighter Engaged, as well as hospitals and disability advocates, to learn about their needs. Thoughtfully and persistently, they began to design a product that would suit every individual's needs.

At one point, it looked like the project was going to be cut due to Microsoft's budget cuts. Johnson and his team rebelled: no matter what happened, they were going to keep working on it. They had a deeper purpose: after countless conversations with their users, they had learned just how important video games are for well-being, how necessary inclusion is, and how much of an impact could be had. Stopping was not an option.

Three years later, their product was revealed: the Xbox Adaptive Controller, a deceptively simple box that can be customized to meet everyone's needs. As one child said, "What I love about the Adaptive Controller is that now everyone can play."

The Adaptive Controller also had a profound impact on the internal team at Microsoft. As Yaron Galitzky, one of the team leaders, said: "I shipped many products. This is the most special product I worked on. The most impactful one . . . Going through this experience just changed our lives. I won't look at products the same way. We are not stopping here. We will take this to more devices, more products."

All told, more than a hundred people within Microsoft brought together their gifts to contribute to the Adaptive Controller project, alongside the many who shared their gifts to inform what was needed. It kicked off a broader movement toward accessibility in Microsoft, shaping new products and services. Johnson now runs Microsoft's Inclusive Tech Lab, the hub for all of this critical work.

The Microsoft team was determined to do the right thing, no matter what. When you are working on the world's problems, there might be times when you, too, have to stand up for what is right. If that happens, focus on your greater purpose—the people you're helping. There's a type of courage that can only be found when you're fighting for other people's well-being. You will be amazed by how powerful it is and how far it will take you.

LESSON #5:
HOPE BUILDS WITH ACTION

In 2007, the entrepreneur Richard Branson and the musician Peter Gabriel approached Nelson Mandela with a big request: Would you like to form a global group called The Elders, to serve as moral leaders and solve the world's toughest problems, like preventing nuclear war,

Your sense of hope will build with every action that you take.

addressing climate change, and establishing peace? And, oh, by the way, will you be the leader?

Mandela was eighty-nine years old at the time. He had already ended apartheid in South Africa, served as president of South Africa, delivered justice through the Truth and Reconciliation Commission, and established a foundation devoted to poverty and HIV/AIDS. Even after all that he had suffered and all that he had given, he said yes, I want to keep helping.

He brought together the most esteemed leaders in the world, including former US president Jimmy Carter, social entrepreneur Muhammad Yunus, and Archbishop Desmond Tutu. Because they hold no public office, The Elders' highest loyalty is to the common good. They use their gifts to bring awareness to suffering, mediate conflicts between governments and people, and advocate for the wisest paths to well-being. Mandela kept doing good for the next six years, until he passed away.

Mandela never lost hope in a better world. Why? Because he never stopped working toward it.

We think of hope as something that happens *to* us, but research shows that hope is really something *you do*. Hope has three components:

- A goal
- The motivation to work toward that goal
- A plan for how you will achieve it

If you find yourself feeling hopeless about the world, follow Mandela's example. Feeling hopeless is not a sign that you should give up. It is a sign that you need to take action.

Refocus on your goal: a happier world. Renew your motivation: the knowledge that working toward it will make you and others happy. And revise your plan: decide on the next step that you can take toward it.

Act, even if it feels hopeless. Act, even if you're scared. Act, even if it seems too small to make a difference. Hope will follow.

LESSON #6:
EMBRACE THE CHALLENGE

From an early age, Suzy Eddie Izzard knew that she wanted to be a comedian. It took years of street performances before she got onto a stage and years more before she got her big break. Eventually, her persistence paid off, with Emmy Award–winning comedy specials and celebrated roles in television, movies, and plays.

Alongside her acting career, Izzard is a humanitarian who sets herself extreme challenges to draw attention to injustice. In 2016, she laced up her running shoes in Mvezo, South Africa, and attempted to run twenty-seven marathons in twenty-seven days in tribute to Nelson Mandela's twenty-seven years in prison; every day, she stopped in at organizations working to carry out his legacy. In spite of a brief hospitalization, which necessitated a double marathon on the last day, she finished her run on schedule and raised £1.3 million for charity.

In 2021, Izzard did the same thing in the middle of the pandemic; this time, on a treadmill, running thirty-one marathons in thirty-one days, ending with a live comedy set in one of the four languages she speaks. She called it her "Make Humanity Great Again" tour.

As a transgender woman, Izzard wants everyone to know that "being your authentic self is great." She uses these ambitious challenges to create a more accepting, loving world. Despite the harassment and vitriol that she receives simply for being herself, she perseveres, knowing that there are people out there whose lives are changed by her work.

Izzard teaches us that we can embrace the challenges in our lives. I am certain that there were so many moments when she wanted to quit running, skip a comedy set, or simply retire from public life so that people would stop treating her cruelly. But she kept going because it mattered.

Changing the world is like a marathon of marathons. You will need to rest and rejuvenate along the way, and you also might have moments when you want to quit. When that happens, say these words to yourself: "This is my contribution to the world, the thing that only I can do. I am choosing this; I can do this; in fact, I was made for this." Then think about Izzard, and get back out on the road.

LESSON #7:
DREAM BIG; START SMALL

Wangari Maathai always has been a trailblazer: she was the first woman in East and Central Africa to earn a master's degree and the first woman to get a doctorate from the University of Nairobi, where she became the first woman to hold an associate professor role and the first woman to become the chair of a department.

In her mid-thirties, she left behind all of these "firsts." Women in rural Kenya were telling her of their troubles: it was getting harder to earn money, find food, gather firewood, and collect water.

Maathai realized that these were signs of a broken relationship between humans and nature. Twelve thousand years ago, before the agricultural revolution began, there were six trillion trees. Less than half remain. In Kenya, British colonialists cleared 90 percent of the forests and forced farmers to degrade their land to produce commercial products.

Maathai realized that it might be possible to heal this relationship. Her idea: restore the well-being of rural women by paying them to plant trees, which would, in turn, restore Kenya's environment.

At first, no one was interested. Undeterred, Maathai started herself, planting a few seedlings in her backyard. After several persistent years of advocacy, she began to gather groups of local women. They nurtured seedlings in cans and cups, moving them to permanent spots to grow tall and strong. Bit by bit, the trees grew and the forest returned. Bit by bit, women discovered their own gifts. Bit by bit, the movement grew.

What started with a few backyard seedlings became the Green Belt Movement, which has now planted more than fifty million trees and helped thirty thousand women. As it turns out, Maathai had

Dream big; start small.

another first in her future: the first African woman to win the Nobel Peace Prize.

Maathai shows us that doing something big always starts with doing something small. In her Nobel Peace Prize acceptance speech, she declared that we must stop destroying that which gives us life and makes all good things possible: our planet. We are called, she said, to help Earth to return to a state of well-being and will discover that this is the only way to return to a state of well-being for ourselves, too. We are called to recognize our deep connections to one another and to honor them with care and compassion. And, she concluded, we are called to elevate our way of thinking once and for all so that we can create a better world where every single creature on the Earth can thrive.

Deep down, I think that we all know she is right. Our time is now. Will we answer the call?

KEY TAKEAWAYS

- No one person will save the world; it will take all of us.

- Identify a global problem that you would like to see addressed. Determine how you can use your gifts to help solve it.

- As you build a happier world, remember these key lessons: be yourself, use your gifts in new ways, reject the status quo, fight for what's right, hold on to hope, embrace the challenge, and dream big but start small.

Conclusion:
The Person in Front of You

In Leo Tolstoy's short story "The Three Questions," a king is passionately searching for the answers to three questions, believing that if he knew them, he could never fail:

- What is the best time to begin everything?
- Who are the best people to listen to?
- What is the most important thing to do?

All of the wisest people in the kingdom came forward to propose their answers, but none satisfied the king. He decided to ask the wise hermit for his perspective. Disguising himself and leaving his bodyguard a short distance away in the woods, he approached the hermit, who was digging beds in his front yard.

The king asked him if he knew the answer to the three questions. The hermit did not reply.

Noticing that the hermit looked tired from digging, the king offered to take up the spade. After digging two beds, he asked the hermit again: do you know the answer to my three questions? Again, there was no response.

Suddenly, a man staggered out of the woods, bleeding from a stomach wound. The king carried him into the hut, placed him on a bed, and cared for him, cleaning and dressing his wound, giving him water, and sleeping on the floor next to him.

When the king awoke the next day, the injured man immediately begged for his forgiveness. He had come to the hermit's house to try to kill the king but had been attacked by his bodyguard in the woods. Then, lo and behold, the king saved his life! The man swore to devote himself to the king's service if he forgave him, which the king did happily.

Before he went back to the palace, the king decided he would ask the hermit just one more time if he knew the answers to his three questions. The hermit, laughing, told him, "You have already been answered!"

"What do you mean?" the king asked.

The hermit explained: When the king saw his own exhaustion from digging the beds, he offered to help, which prevented him from being attacked in the woods by his would-be assassin. Then, when the man stumbled bleeding out of the forest, the king helped him heal from his wounds, which led to their peace.

> "Remember then: there is only one time that is important— and that is now! It is the most important time because it is the only time when we have any power.
>
> "The most necessary man is he with whom you are, for no man knows whether he will ever have dealings with anyone else.
>
> "And the most important thing to do is, to do good, be- cause for that purpose alone was man sent into this life!"

We started this book by exploring three questions of our own: Who am I? What should I do? How am I related to others?

Although our questions are different, they seek out the same ends as the king's questions: the answers that would tell us how to be, what to do, and whom to do it with so that we could find the happiness we longed for. And we arrived at the exact same conclusion that the king and the hermit did: we are here to help each other.

We have gone on a great journey together. In this book, you have learned that you are worthy just as you are and that you have extraordinary gifts within you. You have discovered that those gifts are meant to be used, not to seek outcomes, but as a way of expressing and growing your true self. And you have learned that, because we are all connected, the best way to express those gifts is in service of other people, helping them in the unique, meaningful, enjoyable ways that only you can.

At this point, you might be wondering, "How do I get started?" Tolstoy's fable gives us the answer to this secret, fourth question: start here, wherever you are.

There is a person in front of you. They need you. They need your gifts. They need your help.

And, as it turns out, you need them, too. You need to share your gifts. You need to help them.

Through this shared need, we will help each other find happiness.

Never again wonder if you belong here, if you are needed here, if you have a purpose. Everything you do adds up, contributing to our shared goal of a happier world.

Just as one minute is made of sixty seconds, and one hour is made of sixty minutes; just as the average month is made of thirty days and the years are made of three hundred sixty-five days; so, too, is our world made of individuals. A lifetime may feel countless in its moments, yet it is measurable. Likewise, although there are billions of us in our world, we are measurable, and we all do matter.

As individuals, we can come together, connected by our shared humanity and bound by our new shared goal, and make the world a happier place—one act of help at a time.

Resources

Thank you so much for reading this book. I'd like to share some additional resources that you might find helpful.

References

To explore this book's references, please visit thenewhappy.com /bookreferences.

Tools

To download the tools that were referenced throughout the book, please visit thenewhappy.com/resources.

Bonus Chapters

You can download three additional chapters at thenewhappy.com /bonuschapters:

- Build a Happy Workplace: A guide for leaders who want to help their teams use their gifts at work.
- Use Your Gifts with Your Friends and Family: Practical ways to use your gifts to support your loved ones.
- How to Build Your Resilience and Care for Your Well-Being: Tools and strategies that can help you through difficult life experiences.

Join Our Community

I hope you'll join our community of over a million people who are putting the New Happy philosophy into practice.

Visit thenewhappy.com to get our daily newsletter, podcast, artwork, articles, community challenges, and much more.

Acknowledgments

This book only exists because of the people who helped me.

To Alex—I could write a whole other book describing all you have given to me. This all only happened because, years ago, you looked at me and said, "We can build the better world we dream of, even while ours is crumbling." You gave me unconditional acceptance and true love, which made it possible for me to discover and share my gifts. Thank you for contributing so much of your humanity, wisdom, and talent to this book. It's yours, too.

To my parents—thank you for your extraordinary love and for all that you have given me. I am profoundly grateful to you both, and especially for your encouragement to follow my calling at the age of sixteen and for the countless ways you have supported me since that day.

To Annie—thank you for every thumbs-up, thumbs-down, and question mark; you helped me find my voice.

To Geoff—thank you for talking through many of these ideas with me, debating and encouraging me in equal measure; you gave me the courage to speak up.

To my family, friends, mentors, classmates, and colleagues—you helped me develop this philosophy and share it with the world. You asked important questions, brainstormed with me, offered different perspectives, edited my writing, and suggested new ideas. Your gifts are woven through these pages. I treasure you.

To Lauren Appleton—thank you for believing in the New Happy and turning this book from a dream into a reality. I feel so lucky to have benefitted from your gifts, particularly your constant encouragement, your wise perspectives on life's biggest questions, and your transformative editorial talents. Thank you to the rest of the team at Penguin Random House, especially to Ashley Alliano for your ongoing coordination and assistance.

To Courtney Paganelli—thank you for being a tireless advocate and your steadfast support on this journey. You are such a caring, thoughtful, and brilliant person, and being a beneficiary of these qualities has been a blessing. My deepest thanks to the rest of the team at Levine Greenberg Rostan, especially Stephanie Rostan, Monika Verma, Melissa Rowland, and Miek Coccia.

To the scholars, artists, philosophers, activists, dreamers, humanitarians, visionaries, writers, change-makers, and leaders whose work has shaped the New Happy philosophy—thank you for your humanity, talents, and wisdom. As I wrote this book, I often reflected on the words of Michel de Montaigne, who wrote that "I have gathered a posy of other men's flowers, and nothing but the thread that binds them is mine own." What a joy to have spent the last ten years gathering your flowers; I hope that I have honored you with this bouquet.

To the New Happy community—thank you for giving me the place where I can use my gifts to serve the world. You don't know how much I needed you and how much you helped me, sustaining me through difficult times and bringing me daily joy. The opportunity to serve you is my greatest privilege. You have given me an unshakeable faith in humanity and the absolute certainty that we *can* build a happier world together.

And to you—thank you for reading. I wish you all of the happiness in the world.

About the Author

Stephanie Harrison is the creator of the New Happy philosophy, a groundbreaking new approach to individual and collective happiness. She is an entrepreneur, speaker, writer, and designer. Stephanie's work and expertise have been featured in publications such as CNBC, *Fast Company*, *Forbes*, and *Harvard Business Review*. She is a frequent keynote speaker for Fortune 500 companies.

Stephanie founded The New Happy, a company devoted to helping individuals, companies, and communities apply this philosophy in their lives. The New Happy's award-winning artwork, top-ranked podcast, newsletter, and free behavior-change programs help millions of people in 150 countries around the world.

Prior to The New Happy, Stephanie was the director of learning at Thrive Global, where she led the development of well-being and performance programs. She has a bachelor's degree in individualized studies from New York University and a master's degree in positive psychology from the University of Pennsylvania, where she was later an instructor. She lives in California with her partner, Alex, and their tiny dog, Cleo.